Rise Above

A Stronger Body, A Clearer Mind, A Happier Life

Anthony Punshon

Copyright © 2024 Anthony Punshon
All rights reserved.

No part of this publication may be reproduced, distributed, or transmitted in any form or by any means, including photocopying, recording, or other electronic or mechanical methods, without prior written permission from the publisher, except in the case of brief quotations embodied in critical reviews and certain other non-commercial uses permitted by copyright law.

For permission requests, write to the publisher at:
Office Clerk, C/O Customer Services, Free Box 653, Nexus Connect Esh, Durham, DH7 9QR

Disclaimer
This book is for informational purposes only. It is not a substitute for professional medical advice, diagnosis, or treatment. Always consult with your physician or other qualified health provider regarding any questions you may have about a medical condition or health objectives. The author and publisher assume no responsibility for any adverse effects resulting directly or indirectly from information contained in this book.

ISBN: 9798303703650
First Printing: December 2024
Published by Superalis Publishing

Cover Design: Anthony Punshon
Cover Photo: Sophie Bowden-Caldwell, IC Photographics

Published in Great Britain

For Mum

The very definition of rising above.

Your unwavering strength, kindness, and grace have shown me how to navigate life's challenges with courage and compassion. You've been my role model in every sense—teaching me not just how to face adversity, but how to lift others up along the way. This book wouldn't exist without your example.

Thank you for being my guiding light, my anchor, and my biggest inspiration.

ACKNOWLEDGEMENTS

My Personal Avengers Assemble

This book wouldn't exist without the incredible people who supported me through the highs and lows, the breakthroughs and the breakdowns in my own life. Each in their own way, they were there when I needed guidance, strength, or just someone to remind me I wasn't alone. Each of them played a crucial role in helping me rise above.

To **Laura**, my best friend and the fiercest ally anyone could ask for. You're the person who shows up, sword in hand, even when you're fighting your own battles. When I was at my lowest, you were there—whether it was with practical advice, a listening ear, or just a cup of tea. You've always underestimated how much you mean to the people around you, but let me say it plainly: my life is better because you're in it.

Your support, even during my darkest days, helped me find my way through. You gave me strength when I had none, and I'll never forget that. And of course, your wedding—a day filled with love, laughter, and more fairy lights than a Eurovision performance gone rogue—was the spark that started the journey captured in this book.

Thank you for everything. I couldn't have done it without you.

To **Marisa**, the unexpected hero in my story. That random Pale Man reference at Laura's wedding that you probably don't even remember sparked a connection that pulled me out of a very dark place. Every movie we saw and every event we went to after that was another step out of the pit, and I credit you as the person holding the rope, even though you didn't know it.

I know you're probably all uncomfortable and squirmy as you read this (yes, I'm calling you out), but you need to know how much your friendship has meant to me. We bonded over our shared nerdiness, and I hope we'll keep nerding out together for many years to come.

Thank you for being the friend I didn't know I needed.

To **Sonia**, my long-distance rock and biggest cheerleader. Even though you've moved to the other side of the world, I miss having you close by, but distance has done nothing to dampen your unwavering support.

You've always been a source of strength and encouragement, and recently, you gave me the courage to make a life-changing decision. Your belief in me, even from a bajillion miles away, reminds me that true friendship knows no boundaries.

Thank you for being my champion, my confidante, and my constant source of inspiration. I'm beyond grateful for you.

TABLE OF CONTENTS

Foreword by William Hofacker   1

Prologue:
When Rock Bottom Became Solid Ground   3

Part 1: Mindset—Master Your Mind, Master Your Life

1. The Benefits of Positive Thinking   10
2. The Power of Gratitude   15
3. Finding Calm in Everyday Moments   19
4. Victim Mindset: Reclaiming Your Power   22
5. Forgiveness: Letting Go for Your Own Sake   27
6. The Role of Self-Compassion   31
7. Embracing Risk: Why Playing It Safe Is the Real Failure   35
8. The Power of Connection   39
9. Breaking the Comparison Cycle   44
10. The Ripple Effect: How Helping Others Helps You   48

Quick Wins: Your Cheat Sheet to a Healthier Mindset   53

Success Stories:
From Setbacks to Strength: How Gill Found Her Resilience   57

Part 2: Exercise—Stronger, Fitter, Happier

11. The Movement-Mind Connection   62
12. Walking: The Simplest Path to Wellness   65
13. Metabolic Resistance Training: The All-In-One Workout   69
14. Building Your Personal Fitness Routine   74
15. Tracking Progress Without Obsession   78
16. The Power of Consistency   81
17. Rest and Recovery: Fitness's Secret Weapons   84

Quick Wins: Your Cheat Sheet to a Fitter Body   87

Success Stories:
Stronger Than Yesterday: How Kate Found Her Power, One Step at a Time — 90

Part 3: Nutrition—Eating Well Without Losing Your Mind

18. Healthy Eating Without the Diet Drama — 94
19. Feed Your Brain: Nutrients for Mental Health — 98
20. Protein—Your Body's Unsung Hero — 102
21. Healthy Fats Without the Hype — 106
22. The Fibre Fix: Gut Health and Mental Clarity — 110
23. Hydration Station: Water's Role in Mind and Body — 113
24. Practical Meal Planning Without the Hassle — 116

Quick Wins: Your Cheat Sheet to Guilt-Free Eating — 124

Success Stories:
From Mocha Overload to Morning Miles: How Claire Transformed Her Energy, Health, and Life—One Step at a Time — 127

Conclusion
Soaring Higher: Your Rise Above Toolkit — 131

About the Author — 134

FOREWORD

The Power of Showing Up

By Willam Hofacker

Every so often, a book comes along that doesn't just provide answers—it meets you where you are, equips you with tools, and inspires you to believe that change is possible. This is that book.

I was honoured when Anthony asked me to write the foreword. I expected the book to be good, but what I didn't expect was how much I'd find myself using his strategies to navigate challenges in my own life. That's the power of what Anthony shares in these pages—it's practical, relatable, and transformative for anyone willing to put in the work.

I first met Anthony as his coach, and over time, I've had the privilege of getting to know him as a friend and a fellow member of our book club. What struck me most wasn't just his deep understanding of transformation—it was his ability to live it. Anthony has faced struggles that would leave many people feeling stuck: battling depression, emotional abuse, chronic pain, and the ups and downs of his own health journey. But through it all, he never gave up.

In fact, I witnessed him at his lowest points, showing up—whether to our coaching sessions or book club discussions—with a determination to keep moving forward, even when it felt impossible. The concepts in this book aren't just ideas Anthony teaches; they're principles he's lived by and they're battle-tested.

Anthony's approach is refreshingly down-to-earth. This isn't about quick fixes or chasing perfection—it's about creating balance, resilience, and more joy in your life. Whether it's rethinking how you approach exercise, untangling the drama of nutrition, or rewiring your mindset to embrace gratitude and self-compassion, Anthony breaks it all down into bite sized, actionable steps anyone can take.

What I love most is how Anthony blends science-backed strategies with real-world wisdom and a healthy dose of humour. You'll find yourself nodding in agreement one moment and laughing out loud the next. And perhaps most importantly, you'll feel seen. Wherever you are on your journey, this book will meet you there and help you take the next step.

So, as you dive into these pages, I urge you to embrace the process. I'm certain you'll be glad you did. As you'll learn from Anthony, it's not about doing everything at once—it's about showing up, taking small, meaningful steps, and trusting that those steps will lead to something incredible.

Anthony's story and strategies have already changed so many lives, including mine. I have no doubt they'll do the same for you.

Enjoy the journey.

PROLOGUE

When Rock Bottom Became Solid Ground

There's a little-known battle in the sky, and what happens next could change your life.

Did you know, the crow is the only bird daring enough to peck at an eagle? It'll land on the eagle's back and nip at its neck, trying to drag it down. The eagle, however, doesn't waste time fighting back. It doesn't squawk or flail around in midair. Instead, it spreads its massive wings and begins to soar higher.

You see, the eagle knows a secret: the higher it climbs, the thinner the air becomes. And up there, in the lofty heights where the eagle thrives, the crow struggles. Eventually, the crow can't handle the altitude, and it falls away.

The lesson? Don't waste your time or energy battling every crow that tries to pull you down. Instead, rise above. Focus on your own path, your own growth, and elevate yourself to a place where negativity, criticism, and doubt can't reach you.

This book is called *Rise Above* for a reason. It's about learning how to soar higher, even when life's crows try to drag you down. It's about building the kind of mindset, habits, and resilience that allow you to break free from the things holding you back.

The Day Everything Changed

A year ago, I hit rock bottom. It didn't happen overnight. Life had dealt me a series of blows—months of emotional abuse, relentless stress, and a sense of isolation that slowly eroded my spirit.

Bit by bit, I found myself sinking, until one day I woke up and realised I wasn't just having a rough patch; I was trapped in a pit of depression.

It's the kind of depression where you feel like you're standing at the bottom of a vertical tunnel, surrounded by darkness, with only a faint sliver of light teasing you from above. You know it's there, but it feels unreachable. And you can't just walk out... you have to climb.

Mentally, I was broken. Physically, I was a mess—fat, sluggish, and so far from the fit, energetic person I used to be that I barely recognised myself. My body and mind, once a dynamic duo, had both checked out and left me floundering.

A Wedding and a Spark

Then came my best friend's wedding. It was supposed to be a day about them—celebrating their love, eating cake, and watching distant relatives showcase their 'unique' dance moves. And it was all that, but it was also something more.

Let me paint you a word picture...

My best friend is beautiful in a really classic way. And by classic, I don't mean old... partly because a) it would be hideously untrue (I'm actually convinced there's a painting in her loft that's ageing on her behalf), and b) if I did, she'd knee me so hard in the man-berries, the surgeons would need to remove them from my mouth.

No, by classic, I mean if it was the 1950's her face would be on billboards overlooking a diner, or if it was the 1930s, they'd be painting her on the side of planes. So, when she was in her vintage-looking wedding dress, she looked stunning. The kind of stunning that makes you pause and think, "Is this a wedding, or did I accidentally trip and fall into a Disney cartoon?"

The whole day felt magical, from the twinkling fairy lights (so many fairy lights...) to the idyllic countryside backdrop. It was the kind of event that makes you believe in love, happiness, and the possibility of your life being narrated by Morgan Freeman. You know, it's your life—just way more epic.

But amidst all that joy and celebration, something unexpected happened. I made a connection—a real, human connection—that sparked something inside me. It wasn't grand or dramatic (and I'll talk about this in a later chapter), but it was enough to shift my perspective.

For the first time in months, I felt a flicker of hope. I realised I didn't have to stay stuck in that pit.

One Step, Then Another

The day after the wedding, I did something small but significant: I went for a walk. No fanfare, no grand fitness plan, just one foot in front of the other. And here's something people often overlook—the connection between body and mind. When your body starts to heal, your mind often follows.

Walking wasn't just about movement; it was a step towards reclaiming my mental well-being.

That simple walk became a daily ritual. The fresh air, sunlight, and rhythmic movement were like a gentle balm for my frazzled mind. It reminded me of what I'd always known but had forgotten lately: that a healthier body is a giant leap towards a healthier, happier mindset.

From those walks, I graduated back to the gym. The workouts were gruelling at first—my body protested every squat, every push-up. But with each session, I felt a little bit stronger, both physically and mentally. Slowly but surely, I was climbing out of that tunnel.

From Moving to Mindset

Once I had momentum, I turned my attention to my mindset. I began implementing all those things I'd always preached to my clients but hadn't been practising myself lately. Gratitude journaling, reframing negative thoughts, practising self-compassion—I threw the whole toolbox at it.

But here's the thing: this book isn't about fluffy, feel-good strategies with no grounding. Every technique I used, every hack I discovered, is backed by solid science. Research shows that small, consistent changes in behaviour and mindset can rewire your brain, boost your resilience, and improve your overall happiness.

It wasn't just the old tricks either. I discovered new, evidence-based strategies that became game-changers in my recovery. I learned how to tackle negative thinking head-on, build better habits, and find connection in a world that often feels isolating.

Why This Book?

This book is a collection of everything I used to turn my life around—the tried-and-true methods, the new discoveries, and the habits I've built to keep myself on track.

It isn't meant to be one of those you read, nod along to, and then promptly let gather dust on a shelf while you carry on exactly as you were. You know the type—the ones with great insights but zero follow-through, like a motivational speaker who fires you up but forgets to tell you how to do anything.

Not here, mate.

I've stripped this book down, then stripped it again until all that's left are actionable steps. No fluff, no filler—just pure, unadulterated get-your-life-together gold. You can open this book right now, and I guarantee you'll find at least one thing you can do immediately to boost your health and happiness.

And here's the beauty of it: you can absolutely read this in one go. It's short enough to get through in a weekend (or one particularly long train journey if you're keen). Then, once you've powered through, it becomes your trusty sidekick.

You can dip back in, flip to whatever chapter fits your current struggle, and find something new to action. This book is like a Swiss Army knife for your well-being.

To make things even easier, there's a Quick Wins cheat sheet at the end of each part, giving you a no-nonsense recap and actionable steps—because sometimes, you just need the highlights to get going.

This book isn't about overhauling your entire life in one go. It's about small, doable wins. Like that one friend who shows up, helps you fix a problem, then leaves without judging the state of your living room or the fact you forgot to buy custard creams before they came round.

You can dip in, find what works for you in this moment, and put it into action. Then come back later and do the same with something else.

It's a companion, not a one-night stand. You're not expected to devour it in one sitting, then feel overwhelmed by a mountain of to-dos. Instead, think of it as your go-to toolbox.

Need a mindset boost? Done. Struggling with energy? Sorted. Want to feel more connected to others? Say no more.

Every step fits into your life as it is right now—no crash diets for your brain or 5am kale-smoothie routines required. Seriously, don't overthink it. Pick a chapter, pick a step, and crack on.

Because, let's be honest, changing everything at once is about as realistic as teaching a goldfish to drive. Instead, we'll do it one step at a time.

So, let's get cracking, and remember: progress isn't about being perfect—it's about keeping your momentum going, even if it's just a little shuffle forward today.

Part 1: Mindset

Master Your Mind, Master Your Life

CHAPTER ONE

The Benefits of Positive Thinking

"Every little thing is gonna be alright." - Bob Marley

Let's get this out of the way: I know what you're thinking. Positive thinking? Sounds a bit hippy, doesn't it? The sort of thing that pairs well with dreamcatchers, herbal tea, and wandering barefoot through meadows.

But before you roll your eyes and reach for your scepticism hat, let me assure you—this isn't about pretending life is perfect or singing Kumbaya around a campfire.. No matter how good your tambourine skills are.

Positive thinking is simply about training your brain to focus more on the solutions than the problems.

And yes, I get it. Even the name sounds a bit cringe. If you'd prefer, we can rebrand it—call it "Mental Optimisation," "Brain Boosting," or my personal favourite, "Turbocharged Mindset Engineering." Whatever floats your boat. The point is, this stuff works.

Why Our Brains Love a Bit of Doom

Before we dive into the feel-good science, let's talk about why your brain doesn't naturally lean toward positivity.

Enter **negativity bias**—your brain's unhelpful habit of focusing on the bad stuff like a nosy neighbour peeking through the curtains. This evolutionary quirk once kept our ancestors alive by alerting them to potential threats. Unfortunately, it now has us catastrophising over things like ambiguous text messages and slightly delayed responses.

"Sorry to hear you've gone under."

That was one of the messages waiting for me after I announced I was closing my transformation studio. I blinked at the screen, half-expecting a follow-up offering a shoulder to cry on and a GoFundMe link.

What I'd actually said was simple: "the studio will be closing." No tales of woe, no dramatic declarations of insolvency. Yet, within hours, my inbox was flooded with messages offering condolences and telling me I'd "done well to last as long as I did."

And it's not just me.

A friend of mine, who moved abroad a few years ago, came back to the UK for her sister's wedding. Naturally, instead of asking about the wedding, or even jumping to the obvious scenario that she was on holiday, most people jumped straight to, "So, has it all fallen apart, then? Are you back for good?" Because clearly, attending a sibling's nuptials isn't nearly as likely as fleeing a failed life abroad.

Why do people do this? Why is it so easy to assume that any change must be the result of a disaster?

This is **negativity bias** in action.

Our brains love to fill in the blanks with the worst-case scenario. It's like a faulty car alarm—constantly going off, when someone so much as disturbs the air around it.

The Science of Positive Thinking
But here's the good news: while our brains may lean toward negativity, we can retrain them to focus on the positive. Thanks to **neuroplasticity**, our brains are constantly reshaping themselves based on what we think, feel, and do.

When we actively practise positive thinking, we're strengthening the neural pathways that help us see opportunities, solutions, and, yes, silver linings.

Dr. Barbara Fredrickson's research shows that positive emotions don't just make us feel good in the moment—they broaden our perspective and help us build resources like resilience, creativity, and strong social connections. It's like giving your brain a mental upgrade, opening new doors and possibilities.

On the flip side, negative thinking narrows our focus, keeping us locked into a loop of stress and pessimism. It's as if your brain has a "doom filter" installed, and everything looks a bit more apocalyptic than it really is.

The Benefits of Shifting Your Perspective
Studies show that people who practise positive thinking experience less stress, better physical health, and even longer lifespans. It's like mental fibre—it keeps everything flowing smoothly. (You're welcome for that image!)

And the best part? Positive thinking isn't about ignoring reality or pretending everything's perfect. It's about choosing where to focus your energy and training your brain to be a bit more optimistic.

Practical Ways to Practise Positive Thinking

If you're ready to give this a go, here are some steps to start shifting your mindset:

1. Reframe Negative Thoughts

You're halfway to work when you realise you've left your lunch at home. Instead of grumbling, "Typical, just my luck," reframe it: "Perfect excuse to treat myself to that new café I've been meaning to try." Small mental shifts like this help you break the cycle of negativity.

2. Daily Affirmations

Positive affirmations might sound cheesy, but they're like little pep talks for your brain. Stand in front of the mirror each morning and say something that empowers you. "I'm capable," or if you're feeling adventurous, "I'm the lovechild of a Viking and a superhero, here to crush doubts and conquer kingdoms like a caffeinated squirrel in a nut warehouse." You know, whatever works for you. No judgement here! But whatever you use, say it loud, say it proud.

3. Challenge Your Inner Critic

When your inner doom goblin starts whispering sweet catastrophes in your ear, stop and ask: "Is this thought helpful? Is there any evidence for this?" Nine times out of ten, the answer will be no. Feel free to give that goblin a swift punch in the danglies and move on with your day.

4. Surround Yourself with Positivity

This doesn't mean covering your house in motivational posters of cats hanging from tree branches, but it does mean being mindful of the people and content you engage with. Spend time with uplifting people, watch things that make you laugh, and maybe avoid doom-scrolling through social media late at night.

Action Step: Start a Positivity Journal

Each night, jot down three things that went well or that you're grateful for. They don't have to be big—"I found a parking spot right away" or "The barista smiled at me" counts. Over time, this habit trains your brain to focus on the positive, strengthening those neural pathways.

It's something I've even made a nightly ritual with my son. Before bed, we each take turns sharing three things we're grateful for. Sometimes they're profound—"I'm grateful for our family"—and sometimes they're downright hilarious—"I'm grateful that broccoli isn't dessert." But no matter what, it's a moment of connection and reflection that helps us end the day on a positive note.

If it works for a kid who's often just as grateful for his favourite toy as he is for dodging vegetables at dinner, it can work for you too. Trust me, once you start, you'll be amazed at how quickly the little things begin to add up.

Bottom Line

Positive thinking isn't about ignoring life's challenges; it's about building the mental resilience to face them with a clearer, more optimistic perspective. It's like weightlifting for your brain—it might feel awkward at first, but with practice, you'll get stronger and see the benefits in every area of your life.

So, the next time your brain tries to convince you the sky is falling, calm down there, Chicken Little! Take a deep breath, reframe, and remember: you've got the tools to change your mindset, one thought at a time.

CHAPTER TWO

The Power of Gratitude

"It's a beautiful day, don't let it get away." - U2

Let me tell you a little secret: gratitude is one of the simplest, most effective ways to boost your happiness, and yet, most of us treat it like the dusty exercise bike in the corner of the living room that you hang your clothes on. We know it's good for us, but we can't quite muster the energy to use it.

It's easy to overlook gratitude because it sounds, well, boring. But beneath its humble exterior lies a powerhouse for improving your mental well-being. Practising gratitude isn't about becoming one of those overly cheerful people who clap at the end of a flight; it's about learning to spot the little wins in your day—the ones that often go unnoticed.

We talked about the power of positive thinking and how it helps rewire your brain to focus on what's going right. Gratitude is like the next level of that. It's positive thinking in action, a specific way to reinforce those positive neural pathways we started building earlier.

While positive thinking is about reframing and shifting your perspective, gratitude takes it one step further by actively seeking out and appreciating the good that's already there.

Think of it as the practical application of positivity, a way to turbocharge the mental sunroof we've been working on.

The Science of Gratitude

Gratitude isn't just about saying "cheers" when someone holds the door open. It's about actively recognising and appreciating the good things in your life.

And the science? Oh, it's solid.

When you focus on what you're grateful for, your brain releases dopamine and serotonin—the same chemicals that make you feel warm and fuzzy after hearing your favourite song or finding an accidental curly fry in your basket of chips.

Dr. Robert Emmons, a leading gratitude researcher (see? It's that powerful, it's an actual job!), found that people who regularly practise gratitude experience lower stress levels, better sleep, and improved physical health. It's like giving your brain a well-deserved spa day.

Gratitude in Action: A Daily Habit

You've already heard about my nightly gratitude ritual with my son. What's remarkable is how quickly this simple practice can shift your perspective. Even on the roughest days, it reminds us to find a little bit of light.

Gratitude doesn't have to be complicated or profound. It could be appreciating a warm cup of tea, the sound of rain on the window, or the fact that your socks stayed dry all day. It's about noticing those small moments and giving them the credit they deserve.

Why Gratitude Works

Gratitude works on the same principle as positive thinking, but it gives your brain even more reps in that mental gym.

Gratitude helps strengthen those neural pathways we talked about, making it easier for your brain to automatically look for the good. It's like upgrading your mental puppy from basic obedience to advanced tricks—not only does it fetch the feel-good moments, but it also brings back a cup of tea and a chocolate digestive.

Practical Gratitude Hacks

If you're ready to give gratitude a go, here are some easy ways to make it a part of your daily routine:

1. Keep a Gratitude Journal

Each night, jot down three things that went well. They don't have to be grand—even "I managed to catch my phone with my foot before it hit the floor" counts. Use a notes app if you want to make it even easier—because let's face it, we're glued to our phones anyway.

2. Gratitude Messages

Once a week, send a quick WhatsApp, text, or voice note to someone you appreciate. It could be a friend, a family member, or even the colleague who saved you from an awkward solo ride in the lift. And let's be honest, you didn't want another one-sided conversation about Steve's tortoise and its recent diet change. Sharing gratitude amplifies its effects—for you and the recipient.

3. Gratitude Jar 2.0

You may have heard of a Gratitude Jar where you jot down things you're grateful for on Post-its, and stick them in a jar, then at the end of the year, or whenever you need a boost, you can bust that puppy open for an endorphin boost. If you want to drag that into the 21st Century, forget the traditional jar; create a "Gratitude" album on your phone. Snap pictures of things you're grateful for—a stunning sunset, your pet's hilarious sleeping position, or a freak Chicken McNugget that's (almost) a perfect circle. Seriously, my son had me stop in the street the other day to take a photo of exactly that! On tough days, you can then scroll through your digital jar for a visual reminder of life's little joys.

4. Gratitude Walks
As you walk, mentally list things you're grateful for—the crisp air, a friendly smile from a passerby, or the fact that you didn't trip over that rogue pavement slab and end up performing an accidental breakdance routine for an audience of confused pigeons.

Action Step: Start Small
Tonight, try the gratitude journal. Jot down three things, no matter how small or silly they seem. You'll be surprised at how quickly those little moments add up, shifting your focus and strengthening your mental muscles.

Bottom Line
Gratitude isn't about ignoring life's challenges; it's about building a foundation of positivity that helps you weather them. Start small, stay consistent, and watch how this simple practice transforms your outlook.

Because in the end, it's not about finding a life that's perfect—it's about finding joy in the life you already have.

CHAPTER THREE

Finding Calm in Everyday Moments

"It's the end of the world as we know it, and I feel fine." - R.E.M.

Let's face it: life today feels like a never-ending race, and most of us are sprinting while juggling flaming torches. Between work deadlines, family responsibilities, and the relentless ping of notifications, finding a moment of calm can feel about as achievable as spotting a unicorn in your local Tesco.

But here's the thing—calm isn't some mythical state reserved for monks on mountaintops. It's something you can cultivate in the chaos of everyday life. And the best part? You don't need hours of meditation or a retreat in the woods to get there.

Sometimes, it's about small, intentional moments that help you pause, reset, and keep going without losing your mind.

The Case for Calm

Why does calm matter? For starters, your brain loves it.

When you're stressed, your body activates its fight-or-flight response, flooding you with cortisol and adrenaline. Great if you're being chased by a grizzly bear on a motorbike waving a flaming chainsaw about, but not so helpful when the "threat" is a pile of emails or a passive-aggressive comment in the group chat.

Chronic stress keeps your body in overdrive, which can lead to burnout, anxiety, and a host of physical health issues. Finding calm helps deactivate this stress response, bringing your body back to a state of balance.

Dr. Herbert Benson, a pioneer in mind-body medicine, calls this the **relaxation response**—the opposite of fight-or-flight. Activating it regularly can reduce stress, improve focus, and even lower your risk of chronic illnesses.

Small Calm Moments, Big Impact

The good news is, finding calm doesn't require a complete lifestyle overhaul. It's about weaving small moments of stillness into your day. Think of it as hitting the mental "pause" button, even if just for a few minutes.

Practical Ways to Find Calm

Here are some simple, actionable ways to bring more calm into your life:

1. The 3-Deep-Breath Trick

When stress starts to bubble up, take three deep breaths. Inhale slowly through your nose for a count of four, hold for four, and exhale through your mouth for a count of six. It's like a reset button for your nervous system. Bonus: it works even better if you close your eyes and pretend you're somewhere far away—like a tropical beach hooked up to a piña colada drip, or a magical realm where your inbox deletes itself.

2. The 5-Minute Rule

Give yourself five minutes of quiet time each day. No screens, no distractions, just five minutes to sit, breathe, or even stare out the window like you're in a moody indie music video in the 90s. You'd be amazed at how grounding those moments can be.

3. Find Your Zen Zone
This could be a corner of your house, a bench at your local park, or even your car (parked, obviously). A place where you can escape for a few minutes and breathe. If your "zen zone" involves noise-cancelling headphones and a playlist of whale sounds remixed with lo-fi beats, or the soothing tones of a YouTuber narrating conspiracy theories about cheese, no judgement here.

4. Mindful Mini-Breaks
Next time you're doing something mundane—washing the dishes, waiting for the kettle to boil, or standing in the never-ending queue at the post office—use it as an opportunity to practise mindfulness. Focus on the sensations, sights, and sounds around you. It's like giving your brain a mini holiday in the middle of your day.

Action Step: Start Small
Tonight, try the 3-Deep-Breath Trick before bed. It might feel more unnatural than attempting yoga poses in skinny jeans, but stick with it. Over time, these small moments of calm will start to add up, helping you feel more grounded and less like a human-shaped tornado of stress.

Bottom Line
Finding calm isn't about eliminating stress altogether—life happens, and sometimes it's messy. But by creating space for calm amidst the chaos, you'll build the resilience to handle whatever comes your way.

Because at the end of the day, it's not about being perfect—it's about finding balance. And a little calm can go a long way.

CHAPTER FOUR

Victim Mindset: Reclaiming Your Power

"Why does it always rain on me?" - Travis

We've all had those days where it feels like the universe has personally selected you for some twisted reality show called *How Much Can One Person Take?* You're stuck in traffic, your favourite mug is in the dishwasher, and just as you're about to breathe, you get a passive-aggressive "as per my last email" from Janet in accounting.

By 10am, you're ready to drop to your knees, shake your fists at the sky, and scream, "Why me, Universe? WHY ME?"

Welcome to the **victim mindset**—where every minor inconvenience becomes a cosmic plot against you, and life feels like an endless series of personal attacks. But here's the twist:

often, we're not just reacting to events; we're crafting entire narratives to position ourselves as the star of our own tragic play.

What is the Victim Mindset?

The victim mindset isn't just about having a bad day. It's a way of thinking where you consistently see yourself as powerless, perpetually unlucky, and at the mercy of circumstances. And here's the thing: we don't just react to situations; we actively *construct* stories to cement our victimhood.

Picture this: a friend cancels plans last minute. Instead of accepting that they might genuinely have a conflict, your brain spins a yarn about how they've *always* been unreliable, how you're the one who *always* gets let down. Suddenly, you're not just mildly inconvenienced; you're nailing yourself to your own cross, a martyr in an epic saga of betrayal and abandonment.

The victim mindset thrives on these self-constructed dramas, but here's the problem: the more you rehearse these stories, the more you believe them.

Why We Get Stuck Here

Why do we indulge in this mindset? Because, honestly, it's comforting. It absolves us of responsibility and lets us bask in the warm glow of self-pity. It's like wrapping yourself in a blanket of grievances, telling yourself you're powerless while secretly enjoying the validation.

And don't underestimate the allure of social reinforcement:

"You poor thing, I can't believe they did that to you."

"You've had such bad luck lately; you deserve a break."

While well-meaning, these responses can reinforce the narrative that life is happening *to* you, not because of the choices you make.

The "Let Them" Principle: A Game-Changer

Here's where Mel Robbins's **"Let Them"** principle comes in, and it's a total perspective shift. The idea is simple but profound: *stop trying to control others and let people be who they are.*

Let them misunderstand you.

Let them judge you.

Let them gossip about you.

Let them be "right."

Let them doubt you.

Let them not like you.

This isn't about resignation; it's about liberation. When you stop fighting against how others behave or perceive you, you free yourself from the emotional tug-of-war that drains your energy. You're not surrendering your dignity; you're reclaiming your peace.

For example, if someone decides to run your name through the mud, *let them*. Their gossip says more about them than it does about you. Your job isn't to control their narrative—it's to focus on living your truth.

How the Victim Mindset Affects You (and Others)

Living in a victim mindset doesn't just weigh you down; it impacts the people around you. When you're stuck in this loop, it's easy to become reactive, snapping at loved ones or expecting them to shoulder your burdens.

Maybe you unload your frustrations on your partner after a bad day or ignore your friend's needs because you're too caught up in your own narrative. Over time, this mindset can strain relationships, turning you into the very villain you're so desperate to avoid.

Breaking Free

Shifting out of a victim mindset requires deliberate action. It's about recognising the stories you're telling yourself and choosing to rewrite them. Here's some practical steps to reclaim your power:

1. Flip the Script

When you catch yourself thinking, "Why is this happening to me?" ask, "What can I do about this?" This simple shift turns you from a passive character into the protagonist of your story.

2. Lean Fully Into "Let Them"

Next time someone's actions or words bother you, practise saying, *Let them*. Visualise their behaviour sliding off you like spaghetti off your toddler's spoon onto your white carpet. You don't have to win every battle—sometimes, peace is the real victory.

3. Track Your Wins

Start a "wins" journal. It could be as small as "I didn't scream at Janet today" or "I stayed calm when my neighbour's dog barked for an hour." These moments remind you of your resilience and help you focus on what you can control.

4. Set Boundaries

Taking back control doesn't mean saying yes to everything or everyone. Boundaries are your best friend. They protect your energy and remind you that your time and emotions are valuable. Remember, "No" is a complete sentence. "No, thank you" is a more polite one, but you get the point.

Action Step: Start Small

Tonight, reflect on a recent situation where you felt like a victim. Write down the narrative you created and challenge it like a barrister in a daytime courtroom drama. Slam your fists on the desk and shout 'Objection!' for maximum effect. What was within your control? What could you do differently next time? It might feel as foreign as explaining TikTok to your grandma, but with practice, it gets easier.

Bottom Line

Life will always throw curveballs, but staying in a victim mindset makes every challenge feel like a meteor strike. By embracing the "Let Them" principle and focusing on your own actions, you reclaim your power and free yourself from the exhausting cycle of blame and frustration.

Because at the end of the day, you're not a victim of your circumstances—you're the hero of your own story. And it's time to start owning that role.

CHAPTER FIVE

Forgiveness: Letting Go for Your Own Sake

"Let it go, let it go." - Idina Menzel

Let's talk about forgiveness—a topic that usually divides people into two camps: those who think it's essential for inner peace and those who'd rather wrestle a greased-up crocodile in speedos than let go of a grudge.

To be fair, grudges can be oddly comforting. Like an old, creaky armchair—it's familiar and easy to sink into, even if it leaves you stiff and sore. But here's the thing: while you're settled in, it's quietly leaving its mark on you.

Forgiveness, on the other hand, is like finally standing up, stretching out, and realising just how much better it feels to move on.

The Science of Forgiveness

Forgiveness isn't just a moral high ground; it's a mental health power move.

Research shows that people who practise forgiveness experience lower levels of anxiety, depression, and stress. In fact, a study from the University of California found that forgiveness can improve cardiovascular health. Who knew forgiving your mate for eating the last Pringle could double as heart-healthy cardio?

But forgiveness doesn't mean condoning bad behaviour or forgetting what happened. It's about freeing yourself from the emotional baggage that resentment piles on.

In short, forgiveness is less about the other person and more about lightening your own load.

Why Forgiveness Feels So Hard

Forgiveness feels like waving a white flag, like letting the other person "win." It's as if you're saying, *You hurt me, but I'll let it slide.* And that... Well, that feels unfair. But the truth is, clinging to resentment doesn't punish them; it punishes *you*.

Imagine dragging a suitcase filled with bricks everywhere you go. Resentment is heavy, exhausting, and it only gets heavier the longer you carry it. Forgiveness is like opening that suitcase and chucking out the bricks.

Suddenly, you've got room for things that actually matter—like snacks or, you know... joy.

How Grudges Spill Over

Resentment doesn't stay neatly compartmentalised. It leaks into other areas of your life, often in ways you don't notice. Maybe you snap at your partner for something trivial, or you give a colleague the cold shoulder because they remind you of the person who wronged you.

Grudges are like glitter: once they're out, they get *everywhere*. The longer you hold onto them, the more they spread, affecting your relationships, your mood, and even how you treat yourself.

Practical Steps to Forgive Without Feeling Like a Doormat

1. Write a "Never Sent" Letter
Get everything off your chest by writing a letter to the person who wronged you. Say all the things you've been holding back—the angrier, the better. Then, shred it, burn it, or perform a dramatic reading for your pets. The act of releasing those emotions is surprisingly cathartic.

2. Reframe the Story
Ask yourself, *What can I learn from this experience?* It might be hard at first, but shifting from "Why did this happen to me?" to "What did this teach me?" helps you find meaning and closure.

3. Forgive for Yourself, Not Them
Remember, forgiveness is about you. Picture it as evicting a tenant from your mind who hasn't paid rent in years but still leaves dirty dishes everywhere. You're not doing them a favour; you're reclaiming your space.

4. Practise Self-Forgiveness
We can't talk about forgiveness without addressing the person you're probably hardest on: yourself. If you're carrying guilt over past mistakes, it's time to cut yourself some slack. Repeat after me: *I'm human, I mess up, and that's okay.* Stick around for the next chapter to learn how to do this like a pro.

Action Step: Start Small

Think of a minor grudge you've been holding onto—maybe your partner forgot to put the bins out, or your friend took three weeks to reply to your text. Practise forgiving them. Forgiveness, like any skill, gets easier with practice.

Bottom Line

Forgiveness isn't about excusing bad behaviour or pretending you weren't hurt. It's about taking back your emotional freedom. You're not letting them off the hook; you're letting yourself off the hook—from carrying their mistakes around like a backpack full of bricks.

So, get up from your comfy chair, toss out the glitter, and give yourself permission to move forward lighter, freer, and with a heart that beats just a little bit stronger.

CHAPTER SIX

The Role of Self-Compassion

"Even heroes have the right to bleed." - Five for Fighting

Let's start with a scene most of us know all too well: You've had a bad day. Maybe you missed a deadline, forgot a friend's birthday, or accidentally sent a 3am drunk-text to your boss that was meant for your ex (complete with the opening line "Miss you. What are you wearing?"). Instead of brushing it off, you spiral into self-criticism. *I'm useless. I never get anything right. Why am I like this?*

Sound familiar?

That inner critic—the voice that never misses a chance to kick you when you're down—can feel like it's just part of life. But what if, instead of berating yourself, you offered a bit of kindness?

That's where self-compassion steps in, and trust me, it's a game-changer.

The Science of Self-Compassion

Self-compassion is about treating yourself with the same kindness and understanding you'd offer a friend. It's not about letting yourself off the hook for mistakes; it's about recognising that mistakes are a normal part of life and that beating yourself up won't help you do better next time.

Dr. Kristin Neff, a leading researcher on self-compassion, breaks it down into three components:

1. **Self-Kindness**—Being gentle with yourself rather than critical.
2. **Common Humanity**—Recognising that everyone messes up sometimes; you're not alone.
3. **Mindfulness**—Acknowledging your feelings without getting overwhelmed by them.

Studies show that people who practise self-compassion are more resilient, experience less anxiety and depression, and are better equipped to handle life's challenges. In short, self-compassion isn't just nice to have—it's essential for mental well-being.

Why We're Harder on Ourselves

Here's the thing: most of us find it easier to show compassion to others than to ourselves.

If a friend came to you, upset about a mistake they'd made, you wouldn't tell them they're a complete failure, would you? But when it's your own mistake, that inner critic can sound more like a sugar-fuelled toddler shouting commands as if they're leading a tiny army of chaos.

Why? Because many of us believe that being hard on ourselves is the key to success. We think self-criticism will keep us in line and motivate us to do better. But in reality, it often has the opposite effect, making us more anxious and less likely to take risks or learn from our mistakes.

Rewriting the Inner Script

Let's flip the script. Imagine you're trying to learn a new skill, like dancing or cooking. Which approach do you think would help you improve faster:

- Constantly berating yourself for every misstep and burnt pancake? ("You put it in the pan, give it a bit then turn it over... How hard is that, for crying out loud???")
- Or encouraging yourself to keep trying, even when it doesn't go perfectly? ("Meh, the first one's always a throw-away anyway.")

Self-compassion helps you build a supportive inner dialogue, which makes it easier to bounce back from setbacks and keep moving forward.

Practical Self-Compassion Exercises

Ready to start being kinder to yourself? Here are a few simple ways to practise self-compassion:

1. The Friend Test

Next time your inner critic pipes up, ask yourself: "What would I say to a friend in this situation?" Chances are, you'd offer support and encouragement, not criticism. Try using those same words for yourself.

2. Write a Self-Compassion Letter

Write a letter to yourself about a recent struggle or mistake. Be kind and understanding, just as you would if you were writing to someone you care about. Then, read it back when you're feeling down—it's surprisingly powerful.

3. Affirmations with a Twist
Remember those bold affirmations from earlier? Add a self-compassionate spin: "I'm not perfect, but I'm learning and growing every day," or "I'm doing the best I can, and that's enough." Say them with the passion of a Shakespearean actor reciting their shopping list as if it's the climax of *Hamlet*.

4. Compassion Breaks
When you're feeling overwhelmed, take a moment to pause and acknowledge your feelings. Say to yourself: "This is hard. I'm struggling right now, and that's okay." It's a small gesture, but it can help you reset and move forward with a clearer mind.

Action Step: Start Small
Tonight, reflect on a recent mistake or challenge and try the Friend Test. What would you say to someone else in your shoes? Now, say those words to yourself. Right now it might feel more awkward than running into your ex at the supermarket while in your pyjamas and holding a tub of ice cream the size of a small hatchback, but with practice, self-compassion will become second nature.

Bottom Line
Self-compassion isn't about making excuses or avoiding responsibility. It's about recognising that you're human, and humans aren't perfect. By treating yourself with kindness, you'll not only feel better but also build the resilience to keep growing and improving.

So, the next time your inner critic starts ranting, tell it to sit the hell back down. You've got this—and you deserve a bit of kindness along the way.

CHAPTER SEVEN

Embracing Risk: Why Playing It Safe Is the Real Failure

"Don't stop me now, I'm having such a good time." - Queen

Let's set the scene: You're at a party, and after a few drinks, someone pulls out the karaoke machine. The room buzzes with anticipation as they flip through the songbook, and then it happens—the mic is passed to you.

Your heart races. You know you could absolutely *slay Living on a Prayer*. You've practised it in the shower enough times to make Jon Bon Jovi sound like your mate Dave after four pints and a bad decision.

But instead of grabbing the mic, you freeze. "Nah, I'm good," you mumble, awkwardly waving it off.

Enter Brenda from HR.

She snatches the mic with the confidence of a seagull eyeing your chips and launches into *Dancing Queen*. And by "launches," I mean she sends it crashing into the ground with a performance so off-key it's practically a new genre.

The crowd roars—some from laughter, others from sheer second-hand embarrassment—but Brenda? Brenda doesn't care. She's living her best life, unbothered by the chaos she's created. Meanwhile, you're sitting there, clutching your drink, filled with regret, and muttering to yourself, *"That could've been my moment."*

This, my friend, is the risk paradox. In trying to avoid the discomfort of potential embarrassment, you also miss out on the potential joy, growth, and, yes, even some glorious failure that comes with taking a chance.

Why We Fear Risk
Risk feels scary because it's tied to uncertainty, and as humans, we're wired to avoid uncertainty like Dave avoids his round at the pub.

Your brain thrives on predictability. It likes things to be neat, safe, and boring because that means survival. But here's the thing: while your brain's playing it safe, your potential is gathering dust like a gym membership in February.

In psychology, this fear of risk keeps us in the **comfort zone**—a cosy but ultimately stagnant space. Sure, nothing bad happens there, but nothing great happens either. It's like eating plain toast for every meal. No one's dying from it, but you're also not experiencing the spicy joy of life's figurative sriracha.

The Cost of Playing It Safe
Avoiding risk comes at a price. Over time, the fear of failure leads to regret, missed opportunities, and a life that feels as flat as a portion of chips without ketchup. Every time you say no to a new

challenge, your comfort zone shrinks a little more until even minor risks feel monumental.

Worse, it creates a habit of avoidance. You convince yourself it's better not to try than to risk failing. Soon, you're turning down opportunities faster than a cat swats away affection, all in the name of self-preservation.

Reframing Risk: The Secret Sauce of Growth

Here's the thing: every success story starts with someone taking a risk. Whether it's launching a business, moving abroad, or simply trying out a questionable new hairstyle, the common thread is this—they leapt. And yes, sometimes they belly flopped, but they also learned, grew, and eventually soared.

The secret to embracing risk is changing how you see failure.

Instead of thinking, *What if it all goes wrong?* start asking, *What if this is the start of something amazing?* Even if you fall on your face, you'll be falling forward—and that's progress.

Practical Steps to Embrace Risk

1. Start with Small Risks
You don't have to bungee jump off a cliff towards a pool of rabid piranhas to prove you're brave. Start small: try a bold new recipe, share your ideas in a meeting, or say yes to karaoke (just don't follow Brenda's lead). These small steps build your risk-taking muscles.

2. Set a "Failure Budget"
Give yourself permission to fail a certain number of times. For instance, tell yourself, *I'm allowed three bad singing attempts this month before I start critiquing my skills.* This takes the sting out of failure and turns it into a manageable, even laughable, part of the process.

3. Channel Your Inner Optimist
Instead of catastrophising, flip the script. Ask, *What's the **best** that could happen?* Sure, you might trip on your way to the mic, but you could also bring the house down with a killer rendition of *Bohemian Rhapsody*.

4. Celebrate the Attempt
Whether you crush it or crash and burn, celebrate the fact that you tried. Remember, the crowd may forget the song you sang, but they'll never forget the spirit you brought to the stage (or the dance moves you pulled during the instrumental break).

Action Step: Take One Risk This Week
Pick one area of your life where you've been playing it safe. Take a small but meaningful risk. Maybe it's speaking up in a meeting, signing up for a class, or finally wearing that sequined jacket you've been hiding.

Worst case? You get a funny story out of it.

Best case? You find something new to love.

Bottom Line
Playing it safe might keep you from failing, but it also keeps you from living fully. Growth, joy, and success all live on the other side of risk. So, the next time you're tempted to sit on the sidelines, remember Brenda. She might not have hit a single note, but she stole the show.

And who knows? Your next leap might just be the one that makes you shine.

CHAPTER EIGHT

The Power of Connection

"If you're lost, you can look and you will find me." - Cyndi Lauper

Picture this: a beautiful old barn, draped in hundreds of fairy lights, the kind of setting that feels like a snapshot from a fairytale. It was my best friend's wedding reception, and I was sitting at a long wooden table next to a new friend I'd met just the day before.

We'd spent hours together stringing up those fairy lights, arranging tables, and transforming the venue into something magical. Now, we were sitting back and enjoying the fruits of our labour. She had a glass of wine, I was sipping a diet coke, and we were making small talk about holiday destinations.

That's when I cracked a joke about my skin's inability to handle sunshine. "You know," I joked, "like that guy from *Pan's Labyrinth* with the hands!"

Now, if you're not familiar, *Pan's Labyrinth* is a gothic Spanish fantasy film with enough subtitles to make even the most dedicated cinephile think twice. Niche doesn't even begin to cover it. So when she immediately burst out laughing and replied with her own Pale Man (that's the guy's name) reference, I was genuinely stunned.

Suddenly, what could have been another surface-level conversation to pass the time became a real connection.

It was a tiny moment, but it sparked something in me. For the first time in what felt like forever, I didn't feel trapped in my own head. That random connection pulled me out of the darkness, and as I would later learn, it wasn't just chance—it was science.

Why Connection Matters

We often treat connection as a luxury, something to pursue when everything else is in order. But connection isn't optional—it's essential for mental health. It's not about how many people you know but about those moments where you feel truly seen and understood. Think of it like finding someone who also hates pineapple on pizza. You're not just bonding over a shared opinion—you're connecting on a deeper, almost spiritual level.

In the 1970s, psychologist Bruce Alexander wanted to explore the roots of addiction, so he created what's now known as the **Rat Park experiment**. Previous studies had shown that when rats were kept in isolation with access to drug-laced water, they consistently chose the drugs, often to the point of fatal overdose.

But Alexander had a theory: what if the problem wasn't just the drugs, but the environment?

He created Rat Park, a rodent utopia filled with tunnels, toys, and plenty of rat friends.

The results were astonishing. The rats in Rat Park largely ignored the drugged water, opting instead for regular water and good times with their furry companions. Even rats that had previously been addicted kicked the habit when moved to this enriched environment.

Let that sink in.

Connection and a supportive environment were powerful enough to beat addiction—something we typically think of as a purely chemical dependency. If that's not a mic-drop moment for the importance of connection, I don't know what is.

The Harvard Study

Humans aren't much different from those rats in Rat Park. The **Harvard Study of Adult Development**, which has followed participants for over 80 years, consistently shows that the quality of our relationships is the strongest predictor of happiness and health.

Let's break that down: it's not the size of your bank account, the number of followers on your social media, or even how many abs you can count in the mirror. Nope. The secret sauce to a fulfilling life is who you've got in your corner. Your relationships are the VIP pass to a healthier, happier you.

Think of relationships as your personal life coaches. They're there to cheer you on when you're smashing your goals, console you when you've face-planted into a metaphorical (or literal) mud puddle, and occasionally roast you with love when you really need it.

And it's not just about emotional support—relationships have physical benefits too. Good friends and strong family ties are like the multivitamins of life. They help you live longer, reduce the risk of chronic diseases, and even keep your brain sharp as you age. It's like having a personal trainer for your soul who also knows how to make a killer cup of tea.

Imagine your relationships as an emotional bungee cord. When life yanks you off a cliff—whether it's a breakup, a job loss, or a disastrous haircut—they're the ones who pull you back up before you hit rock bottom. Without them, you're free-falling, and spoiler alert: the ground's not made of pillows.

So, while it's tempting to chase the next shiny thing—be it a promotion, a flashy car, or the perfect Instagram post—remember that your real wealth is sitting right there next to you on the sofa, probably hogging the popcorn during movie night.

Why Social Media Isn't Enough

But here's the twist: we're more connected than ever through technology, yet more isolated than ever in reality. Social media creates the illusion of connection, but it's like eating a microwave meal that looks amazing on the box but comes out soggy and sad.

The endless scrolling, the carefully curated highlight reels, the "likes" and comments—they don't provide the depth of face-to-face interaction. Instead, they often leave us feeling more isolated and stuck in a cycle of comparison (more on that in Chapter 9).

Practical Steps to Build Real Connection

1. Prioritise Face-to-Face Time
Meet up with friends or family in person. Whether it's over a cup of coffee, a walk, or a shared meal, these moments of real interaction are invaluable for your mental health. Yes, even if it means actually putting on trousers.

2. Join a Community
Find a group that aligns with your interests, whether it's a local book club, fitness class, or hobby group. Even if it's a club for people who knit outfits for their houseplants, shared activities foster consistent, meaningful connections.

3. Volunteer Your Time
Helping others is a surefire way to strengthen your sense of connection and purpose. It benefits both the community and your mental well-being. Plus, it's a great excuse to escape Brenda from HR's endless cat stories.

4. Unplug to Reconnect
Set aside time each day to step away from your phone and engage fully with the people around you. Trade doom-scrolling for something more wholesome, like people-watching at a café or debating whether oat milk is worth the hype. Spoiler: It is.

Action Step: Reach Out
This week, think of one person you haven't connected with in a while. Send them a message and arrange to meet up. It could be as simple as grabbing a coffee or going for a walk.

And no, this doesn't mean a passive-aggressive "we should catch up sometime" message. Be specific!

Notice how even a small interaction can brighten your day and strengthen your mental well-being.

Bottom Line
That conversation in the barn wasn't earth-shattering on its own, but it reminded me of something crucial: connection, in its simplest forms, is life-changing. Whether it's a shared laugh about an obscure movie or a deep heart-to-heart, these moments tether us to something bigger than ourselves.

So, think about your connections. Who can you reach out to today? Because sometimes, all it takes is a shared joke about a creepy guy with eyeballs in his hands to remind you that you're not alone.

CHAPTER NINE

Breaking the Comparison Cycle

"Why can't I be you?" - The Cure

We've all been there. You're scrolling through social media, and suddenly, you're hit with it: *comparisonitis*. (That's a real word. Probably...)

Your old schoolmate has just bought a house that looks like it came straight out of *Grand Designs*. Someone else is showing off their perfect holiday snaps, all glowing tans and infinity pools. Meanwhile, you're sitting there in your mismatched pyjamas, eating cold toast and wondering where it all went wrong.

It's human nature to compare. We want to know how we're doing relative to everyone else. But when those comparisons are based on curated highlight reels, we're playing a losing game. You're comparing your blooper reel to someone else's Oscar-worthy performance.

Why We Fall Into the Comparison Trap
Comparison used to be simple. You'd look over your neighbour's fence, see they had a slightly greener lawn, and think, *I should water my grass more.* But now, with social media, it's like staring at the world's most perfectly manicured garden while your lawn is on fire and a gnome is slowly sinking into the mud, waving a tiny white flag from his fishing rod, with a single porcelain tear rolling down his cheek.

We compare because we're constantly exposed to other people's lives in a way that humans never were before. And it's not just their lives; it's their *best* lives. Filters, edits, and carefully chosen angles mean you're seeing the fantasy version, not the reality. It's like watching a rom-com and assuming that's what every relationship should look like—cue dramatic airport chases, sentimental speeches in the pouring rain, and impromptu musical numbers on public transport.

The Psychological Toll
Comparison doesn't just make you feel bad in the moment. It rewires your brain to focus on what you lack, rather than what you have. It's like driving a convertible along a scenic coastal road, but instead of soaking in the ocean views and golden sunsets, you're laser-focused on every pothole. Not only are you missing the beauty, but you're also one distracted moment away from steering straight into the sea.

Studies show that frequent social comparisons can lead to higher levels of anxiety, depression, and even envy-induced rage. You know, the kind of irrational anger that makes you want to set your phone on fire and ceremoniously hurl it into the nearest volcano.

Worse, this habit creates a vicious cycle.

The more you compare, the worse you feel, and the worse you feel, the more you compare. It's like being stuck on a nightmare merry-go-round, except instead of whimsical horses, you're riding judgmental flamingos, and they're all sneering at your life choices.

Flipping the Script: The Power of Positive Input

Here's where things start to turn around. If negative input fuels the comparison trap, then positive input is your way out.

Think of your mind like a garden. If you constantly dump in trash—gossip, doom-scrolling, reality TV marathons featuring people yelling about who drank the last kombucha—your garden will look like a landfill. But feed it with good stuff—uplifting content, inspiring people, actual sunlight—and you'll start to see some growth.

Curate your digital diet like you'd curate a buffet. Follow people who inspire, educate, or genuinely make you laugh. Fill your feed with content that lifts you up, not drags you down. Unfollow or mute anyone whose posts make you feel like you're not enough.

Remember, you're the gatekeeper of your own mental space.

Practical Steps to Break the Comparison Cycle

1. Audit Your Social Media

Spend some time going through your social media. Ask yourself: *Does this person's content inspire me, or does it make me feel worse about myself?* If it's the latter, hit unfollow faster than you'd close your browser after accidentally opening *that* Incognito tab at work.

2. Limit Your Screen Time

Set boundaries. No more doom-scrolling before bed or waking up to a flood of curated perfection. Instead, start or end your day with something uplifting—a book, a walk, or sitting in the garden pretending to be a wise philosopher while sipping tea.

3. Focus on Your Own Wins

Keep a journal of your achievements, big or small. Did you crush a work presentation? Finally fold that mountain of laundry? Celebrate it. You're the star of your own show, and your victories deserve a standing ovation (even if it's just from your cat).

4. Connect with People Offline
Nothing beats real-life interaction. Meet up with friends, join a local group, or even strike up a conversation with Brenda from HR about her latest cat-themed escapade. When you're busy building genuine connections, you'll find less time to worry about what others are posting online.

Action Step: Take a Digital Detox
Pick one day this week to go completely offline. Don't be scared—it's not like you're cutting off a limb. You'll survive, and who knows? You might even enjoy it.

Use that time to do something you love—read, cook, paint, or even dance around your living room like nobody's watching. Pay attention to how much lighter you feel without the constant influx of curated content.

Bottom Line
Comparison may be human, but it doesn't have to rule your life. The next time you catch yourself spiralling, remember this: someone else's highlight reel doesn't invalidate your reality. You're doing just fine, mismatched pyjamas and all.

So, step off the flamingo carrousel, take a deep breath, and focus on your own journey. Because, honestly, cold toast and all, your life is pretty fantastic.

CHAPTER TEN

The Ripple Effect: How Helping Others Helps You

"Take my hand, we'll make it I swear." - Bon Jovi

Let's get one thing straight: helping others isn't just about being a saint or chasing after some elusive karma points like you're collecting stamps on a loyalty card for the afterlife. The real magic lies in the fact that science shows helping others is one of the best things you can do for your own mental health.

You've probably heard the old saying, "It's better to give than to receive." Sounds like something your nan would mutter while handing you a pair of socks for Christmas. But as cliché as it may be, research proves this sentiment isn't just hippie nonsense. Studies have shown that acts of kindness don't just make the recipient feel good—they light up the giver's brain like a Christmas tree on steroids.

Imagine this: you stop to help someone pick up a stack of papers they've just scattered across the pavement. At that moment, your brain is flooded with oxytocin, the "bonding hormone," dopamine, the "reward hormone," and serotonin, the "happy hormone." It's like your internal chemistry set just whipped up the perfect cocktail of good vibes. You walk away feeling like you've just unlocked a secret level of humanity, strutting down the street like a benevolent superhero.

And the best part?

You don't need to pull off grand, self-sacrificing gestures to get these benefits. Simple acts of kindness—like holding the door open for someone or complimenting their questionable choice of socks—can work wonders for your mood and overall well-being.

Why Helping Others Feels So Good

Let's break this down. When you help someone, your brain doesn't just give you a polite pat on the back—it rolls out the red carpet and throws a full-blown parade in your honour. That hormone rush I talked about earlier? That's the whole squad of feel-good hormones showing up like it's a festival and the water isn't 5-quid a bottle.

But it's not just about the chemical party in your head. There's also a deeper, evolutionary reason behind why helping others feels so good.

Back in the day, when we were all wandering around in loincloths and trying not to get eaten by sabre-toothed tigers, cooperation was essential for survival. You looked out for your tribe, and they looked out for you. Lending a hand wasn't just nice; it was life or death.

Fast forward to today, and while we're no longer fending off predators with sticks (unless you count Janet from Accounting's passive-aggressive emails), that same evolutionary wiring is still there.

Helping others taps into a primal sense of purpose, reminding us that we're part of something bigger. It's why even small acts of kindness—like giving up your seat on the bus or sharing your umbrella in the rain—can make you feel warm and fuzzy inside.

And here's the best bit: helping others can even reduce your own stress levels.

Studies have found that people who regularly engage in acts of kindness report lower levels of anxiety and depression. It's like a psychological boomerang—the kindness you put out into the world comes back to you, improving your own mental health along the way.

The Helper's High

There's even a term for this post-helping glow: the **helper's high**. Think of it like a runner's high, but without the inconvenient side effects of sweating and wondering why you thought running was a good idea.

It's that warm, fuzzy feeling you get when you know you've made someone's day a little bit brighter.

And it's not just a fleeting boost. Research shows that people who regularly perform acts of kindness have lower blood pressure, experience less chronic pain, and even live longer. In other words, helping others is like a supercharged multivitamin for your soul—except it's free and doesn't taste like chalk.

The Ripple Effect

Here's where it gets really interesting. Kindness is contagious. When you help someone, they're more likely to help others, creating a ripple effect of positivity. It's like tossing a pebble into a calm pond—except instead of ripples of water, you're creating ripples of goodwill that spread far beyond what you can see.

Imagine a world where everyone paid it forward.

Someone holds the door for you, and later that day, you let someone merge in front of you during rush hour. That person goes home and offers to do the dishes for their partner, who, in turn, surprises their kids with an impromptu trip to the park. Before you know it, your one small act of kindness has sparked a chain reaction that brightens dozens of lives.

Practical Steps to Start Helping Others

1. Start Small
You don't have to volunteer for a year-long mission to Antarctica, learning to knit jumpers for penguins in sub-zero temperatures to make a difference. Small acts of kindness, like taking your overwhelmed mum friend's kids out for the afternoon so she can have some well-needed me-time, or paying for the coffee of the person behind you in line, can have a huge impact.

2. Volunteer Locally
Find a cause that resonates with you. Whether it's working at a food bank, walking dogs at an animal shelter, or tutoring kids, giving your time and skills is one of the most rewarding ways to help. Bonus: you'll probably meet some amazing people along the way.

3. Be a Listener
Sometimes, the best way to help someone is simply to be there for them. Lend an ear when a friend needs to vent, or check in on someone who's been going through a tough time.

4. Pay It Forward
Make a habit of doing one random act of kindness each day. It could be as simple as leaving a kind note for a colleague or letting someone go ahead of you in the queue at the supermarket. These small gestures add up and can inspire others to do the same.

Action Step: Choose Your Kindness Challenge
This week, pick one way to help someone and make it your mission. Maybe it's volunteering, or perhaps it's as simple as surprising a friend with their favourite snack. Notice how doing something for someone else lifts your own spirits—it's like a two-for-one deal on happiness.

Bottom Line
Helping others doesn't just make the world a better place; it makes *you* a better, happier person. The next time you're feeling a bit low, try reaching out to help someone else. You might just find that lifting someone else up gives you the boost you needed all along.

So, what's your first move? Because in the game of life, the best way to win is by helping others level up too.

QUICK WINS

Your Cheat Sheet to a Healthier Mindset

You've made it through Part 1, and now it's time to bring everything together. Whether you're here to refresh your memory or jump straight into action, this cheat sheet will get you up and running—no need to re-read the whole section (though, I mean, why wouldn't you?).

Key Concepts Recap

- **Positive Thinking: Yes, It Sounds Hippy, But Stick with Me**
  Look, I get it. The idea of "thinking positively" might sound like something you'd hear from a tie-dye-clad guru at a wellness retreat. But this isn't just wishy-washy nonsense; it's backed by science. Focusing on solutions rather than problems literally rewires your brain, strengthening its

ability to handle stress and setbacks. Think of it as a mental gym—except no one's judging your form.

- **Gratitude: Train Your Brain to Spot the Good**
  Gratitude is like the highlighter pen of life. It helps you focus on the wins, no matter how small. Start noticing and appreciating these moments, and suddenly, the world feels a bit brighter—even if it's just because you managed to brew your tea without the bag splitting.

- **Affirmations: Hype Yourself Up**
  If you're imagining someone staring into a mirror chanting, "I am the master of my destiny," I hear you. But affirmations are more than cheesy mantras. They're a way to rewire your brain by focusing on what you want to achieve. Whether it's "I've got this deadline handled" or "I'm basically a productivity wizard," affirmations can help shift your mindset from doubt to determination.

- **Self-Compassion: Be as Kind to Yourself as Brenda in HR Is to Her Cats**
  We all mess up. But instead of beating yourself up, try cutting yourself some slack. Self-compassion isn't about making excuses; it's about treating yourself with the same kindness you'd offer a friend. After all, you wouldn't tell your mate they've failed at life because they forgot to defrost the chicken, would you?

- **Victim Mindset: Ditch the Narrator of Doom**
  Sometimes life kicks you in the proverbial man-berries. But wallowing won't help. Reframe your narrative—are you a passive player in life's soap opera, or are you the underdog hero, ready for a comeback montage? Spoiler: You're the hero.

- **Forgiveness: Drop the Emotional Baggage**

Forgiveness isn't about letting someone off the hook; it's about freeing yourself from carrying their wrongdoings like a backpack full of bricks. Let go, not for them, but so you can walk lighter and enjoy the journey ahead.

Action Steps

1. **Gratitude Practice**
   Each night, jot down three things you're grateful for. They don't have to be monumental—"The barista got my coffee order right" or "My socks actually match" are wins worth celebrating. Bonus points if you manage to do this without rolling your eyes.

2. **Craft and Use Affirmations**
   Write affirmations that speak to your goals and say them daily. No need to go full *Lion King* sunrise chant, but a simple, "I can handle whatever today throws at me" works wonders. For extra impact, throw in a superhero pose—because why not?

3. **Challenge Negative Self-Talk**
   When your inner critic starts up, tear their case apart like you're in a courtroom drama. Stand up, slam your imaginary briefcase on the table, and yell, "Objection!" Replace the negative thought with a more balanced, constructive one.

4. **The Forgiveness Letter**
   Write a letter to the person you're holding a grudge against. Pour out all the emotions, then ceremoniously destroy it. Shred it, recycle it, or go full-on drama and burn it (safely, of course). Feel the weight lift as you let go.

5. **Pause and Reframe**

When things go wrong, take a breath and ask, "What's the lesson here?" It might sound a bit 'zen master,' but reframing challenges as opportunities for growth helps you move forward with a clearer, more positive mindset.

Final Pep Talk

Congratulations—you've got a toolbox brimming with practical strategies to supercharge your mindset. Remember, you don't have to do it all at once. Pick a couple of steps, make them a habit, and watch the momentum build.

So, give yourself a mental fist bump, crank up some classic Bon Jovi, and let's move on to Part 2. Things are just getting started.

SUCCESS STORIES

From Setbacks to Strength

How Gill Found Her Resilience

Growing up in Yorkshire as the youngest of three girls, I was always actively involved in sports and exercise until a car accident changed everything. Before long, my physical health was pretty poor. I did a lot of walking but no other exercise, and my mental health was a rollercoaster of good and bad days.

I was constantly feeling lethargic and struggling to manage life and work. One day, I looked in the mirror and didn't recognise myself. That's when I knew I had to make some changes to my lifestyle.

I started with my diet, making significant adjustments. I controlled my portion sizes, increased my protein intake, cut out snacking on sweets and crisps, reduced carbohydrates, and cut down on alcohol. Before, my diet was generally healthy, with home-cooked meals and wine on weekends, but work travel meant I often ate hotel and restaurant food. Now, I follow a routine of high-carb days, low-carb days, and allow myself a cheat day. I also stopped comfort eating under pressure.

I noticed that ultra-processed foods, daily bread, and sugary snacks negatively affected my mood and mental clarity. On the other hand, increasing my water intake, reducing bread, and choosing healthier snacks like protein bars and cucumber with hummus had a positive impact.

Handling challenges was about not being too hard on myself. If I had a setback, I'd get back on track quickly, reminding myself how good I felt when I stuck to my plan. Planning meals and snacks for the week helped a lot.

For exercise, I embraced MRT (Metabolic Resistance Training) classes, which was a big change since I'd never done MRT before. I used to only go to the gym when staying in hotels. Now, I attend two or three MRT classes and circuits weekly and often add another MRT session or home exercises. I walk daily instead of driving short distances and introduced lunchtime walks. These routines boost my mental health significantly. Exercising early in the morning, especially the 5:45am class, sets a positive tone for the day and improves my resilience. Lunchtime walks help break up my sedentary job and give me a clear perspective on my tasks.

Initially, my achievements were weight loss and increased muscle, but soon I started to feel like myself again. I had more energy and coped better in stressful situations. A milestone for me was studying for my MSc while working full time. I noticed that exercising and sticking to my diet improved my energy levels during lessons and assignments, and my productivity at work increased without procrastination.

The benefits of regular exercise kept me motivated. I became more focused, calmer, and better at handling pressure. It took about two months to notice these improvements, but managing stressful situations and sleeping better were some of the unexpected benefits. I experienced improved sleep quality, sustained energy, and felt stronger and more like myself, which boosted my confidence.

While studying for my MSc and working long hours with significant travel, I noticed my ability to process new information increased, and I could handle difficult situations better. I had more energy and engaged in more activities instead of lounging in front of the TV. I wasn't as sleepy and didn't fall asleep during movies anymore.

To anyone considering making similar changes, I say: do it. Find an exercise you enjoy and can fit into your lifestyle. Build it into your routine until it becomes a habit and part of your life. You won't regret it, and your resilience will improve significantly. Remember, diet and exercise should be healthy, not restrictive, because you're feeding both your mind and body.

My support system played a huge part in my journey. My husband, family, friends, trainer and coach (Anthony), and gym buddies were incredibly supportive. Walking into the gym and feeling welcomed by the trainer and everyone there made it enjoyable. My friends noticed the changes in me and encouraged me to continue and share what I was doing. Their support, encouragement, and compliments kept me going.

I hope to maintain my exercise programme and healthy eating long-term. Online Zoom classes and recorded sessions help keep me on track. Currently, I'm unable to exercise due to an injury and really miss the physical and mental benefits. But I know this is short-term, and I'll return to exercise, starting with physio and building back up to MRT classes. I miss the resilience and mental health boost that exercise gives me.

The most crucial factors in my journey were finding the right gym with like-minded people, enjoying the MRT classes, and fitting them into my lifestyle. My husband's support made healthy eating part of our routine without calling it a diet. Seeing and feeling the changes in my resilience and confidence has motivated me to maintain these habits.

Part 2: Exercise

Stronger, Fitter, Happier

CHAPTER ELEVEN

The Movement-Mind Connection

"Running' up that road, be running' up that hill" - Kate Bush

We've all heard the saying, "Healthy body, healthy mind," often from someone who starts their day with a green smoothie and more enthusiasm than your coffee-deprived soul can handle.

But here's the thing: science actually backs it up.

Physical activity isn't just about chiselling your abs or running faster than your mate Dave runs to the toilet when it's his round. It's one of the most powerful tools you have to improve your mental health.

How Exercise Works Its Magic on Your Mind

When you exercise, your brain lights up like the IT helpdesk when Janet from Accounting tries to open a PDF. Chemicals like endorphins, serotonin, and dopamine flood your system, creating a natural high that even the best double-shot espresso can't rival.

These are your mind's cheerleaders, complete with glitter cannons and a backflip off the judge's table.

Then there's neurogenesis—fancy-pants science speak for "growing new brain cells." Regular movement actually helps your brain grow and adapt, improving memory, learning, and problem-solving. Who knew squats could make you smarter?

And... yes, we're not done... there's cortisol. This stress hormone, when left unchecked, turns you into a bundle of nerves held together by sheer willpower and a fraying shoelace. Exercise helps regulate cortisol, keeping you calm, cool, and far less likely to shout at Brenda in HR when the printer jams (again).

Why Sitting Still Won't Solve It

Now, you might be thinking, "But I'm mentally exhausted; shouldn't I just rest?" And while rest is crucial (more on that later), staying glued to your sofa won't do your mind any favours. Studies have shown that sedentary behaviour—aka becoming one with your Netflix queue—can actually increase symptoms of anxiety and depression.

It's not about running marathons or bench-pressing a baby elephant. Even small amounts of movement can have a massive impact on your mental health. A brisk 10-minute walk can be enough to lift your mood, like hitting the mental reset button after a long day.

Practical Steps to Get Moving

1. Start Small
Forget signing up for a triathlon right out of the gate. Begin with manageable goals—walk around the block, stretch during TV ads,

or dance around your kitchen like no one's watching (bonus points for air guitar).

2. Find What You Enjoy
If you hate running, don't run. If yoga makes you want to scream, skip it. The best exercise is the one you actually want to do. Whether it's swimming, cycling, or chasing your dog around the park, find something that gets you moving and makes you smile.

3. Buddy Up
Exercising with a friend not only keeps you accountable but also adds a social boost. Plus, there's nothing like a good laugh when your mate tries to do a plank and ends up faceplanting with the grace of a falling wardrobe.

4. Set a Routine
Schedule your workouts like you would any other appointment. Pencil it in, set reminders, and treat it as non-negotiable time for your mental and physical health.

Bottom Line
Exercise isn't just about building a stronger body; it's about creating a stronger mind. Each step you take, every drop of sweat, is an investment in your mental well-being. So, whether you're smashing out squats or simply strolling around the block, remember—you're not just moving your body, you're moving your mind forward.

CHAPTER TWELVE

Walking: The Simplest Path to Wellness

"And I would walk 500 miles." - The Proclaimers

Let's rewind to the beginning of my journey back to wellness. I didn't start with an intense workout plan or a meticulously crafted diet. No, my first step—both literally and figuratively—was a simple walk.

I knew walking could help, but convincing myself to get off the sofa? That took a pep talk worthy of a sports movie montage. Trainers on, deep breath, out the door.

And here's why that first step matters: walking is one of the simplest, most effective ways to improve both your physical and mental health.

Why Walking Works Wonders

Walking often gets dismissed because it's so basic. But don't let its simplicity fool you. It's a low-barrier, go-at-your-own-pace kind of exercise with a bucket-load of benefits.

Physically, it gets your heart pumping, your muscles working, and can even help you shift those extra pounds. How? By boosting something called NEAT—Non-Exercise Activity Thermogenesis. Basically, it's all the calories you burn doing everyday stuff that isn't formal exercise. Walking, fidgeting, even wildly gesticulating while you tell a story—it all adds up.

Think of NEAT as the sneaky sidekick of your metabolism, quietly burning through calories while you're just out living your life. So, every time you choose to walk instead of slouch, you're giving your metabolism a gentle nudge, like a mate saying, "Go on, just one more shot"—except this time it's in the name of health.

Mentally, walking is like hitting the refresh button on your brain. It gets those feel-good chemicals—endorphins, serotonin, dopamine—flowing, turning your mind from a gremlin with a bad hangover into a dog hearing the word 'walkies.'

It's also a secret weapon for creativity. Studies show that walking boosts your problem-solving skills and helps you think more clearly. Ever notice how the best ideas pop up when you're moving? It's like your brain's saying, "Ah, finally, some fresh air and blood flow—let's get to work!"

Plus, there's the stress-busting power of walking. It helps dial down cortisol, your body's built-in panic button, so you're less likely to lose it when someone uses the last of the milk and puts the empty carton back in the fridge.

From Casual Strolls to Mindset Shifts
Walking isn't just about moving your body; it's about shifting your mindset. When I first started, I wasn't thinking about calorie burn or fitness milestones. I just wanted to feel human again—and let's

be honest, less like a fuming kettle about to blow and more like someone who could handle a conversation without snapping like a breadstick.

It's funny how the simplest things—like putting one foot in front of the other—can work magic. One minute you're trudging along, convinced the world is out to get you; the next, you're halfway through your walk, solving life's mysteries like Poirot, impeccably dressed and twirling a magnificent moustache.

Suddenly, that awkward moment when you accidentally waved back at someone who wasn't waving at you doesn't seem like the end of the world, and maybe, just maybe, you'll survive another day without screaming into a pillow.

Walking has this sneaky way of helping your brain sort through the clutter. It's like a personal assistant you didn't know you had, tidying up your thoughts while you enjoy the scenery.

Problems shrink, solutions appear, and by the end of it, you're practically ready to deliver a TED Talk on how to conquer life.

Practical Steps to Start Walking

1 Make It a Habit
Start small—maybe a 10-minute walk around your neighbourhood. Gradually increase the time as it becomes part of your routine. Think of it as proving to your smug smartwatch that you're more than just a glorified couch ornament.

2. Find Your Pace
Don't stress about speed. Whether you're sauntering like you're casing the joint or power-walking like you've just spotted your ex across the street, just keep moving.

3. Walk with Purpose

Whether it's to clear your head, catch up with a friend, or practise your 'top of the morning!' wave to unsuspecting strangers, give your walks a purpose beyond just exercise.

4. Combine Walking with Mindfulness
Leave your phone behind (or at least put it on silent) and focus on the sights, sounds, and sensations around you. If you can manage not to check your phone for a full 20 minutes, you deserve a medal—or at least a smug sense of superiority.

5. Track Your Progress
If you're motivated by numbers, use a step counter or an app to track your daily walks. Watching those steps add up can be surprisingly satisfying, like hitting a streak on a fitness app without lying to yourself about those "gentle stretches."

Bottom Line
Walking isn't just about putting one foot in front of the other; it's about putting your mental health in the fast lane. It's cheap, it's easy, and it doesn't require Lycra (unless you're into that sort of thing).

So, lace up those trainers, take a deep breath, and hit the pavement. Whether you're walking for fitness, mental clarity, or just to escape the chaos of modern life, every step counts.

CHAPTER THIRTEEN

Metabolic Resistance Training: The All-In-One Workout

"You've got the touch, you've got the power!" - Stan Bush

A couple of days after the wedding, I was sitting on my sofa, half-watching god-knows-what on Netflix, when I happened to glance down.

There it was: my dad-bod, staring back at me in all its pasty, squishy glory. Fat rolls, zero definition—I looked like Jabba the Hutt had a lovechild with a deflated balloon.

I'd known I was out of shape, but that was my wake-up call.

I shuffled to the bathroom, stepped onto my fancy-pants scales—the kind that measures body fat—and braced for impact. Although I weighed just 128 pounds, my body fat was over 20%. To put that into perspective, 15% is considered good shape, with athletes sitting at 13% or lower (for men). Not only was I carrying more fat than I was comfortable with, but I also had next to no muscle tone.

I wasn't just a dad-bod cliché; I was the actual poster-boy for it.

I had a lot of work to do. But as a trainer, I knew exactly where to start: Metabolic Resistance Training (MRT).

It wasn't going to be easy, but I committed to it. And sure enough, with consistency and determination, I cut my body fat in half, ditched the dad-bod, and—brace yourself—saw my abs again.

Let's break down why MRT works and how it can transform not just your body, but your entire outlook on fitness and mental health.

What Makes MRT So Special?

Metabolic Resistance Training combines strength training with cardio in a beautifully efficient package. Instead of spending hours on separate workouts, you're getting the best of both worlds in one session.

Think of it like riding a unicycle while juggling your morning coffee and a bagel—chaotic but impressively efficient. MRT works by keeping your heart rate up while challenging your muscles, turning you into a calorie-burning machine during and long after your workout.

Here's where it gets science-y (but stay with me): MRT cranks up your Excess Post-Exercise Oxygen Consumption (EPOC). That's a fancy-pants way of saying your body keeps burning calories like a furnace even after you've collapsed on the sofa, smugly scrolling through memes about how hard you crushed it.

The Mental Benefits: Flex Your Brain, Too

Now, let's talk about your brain. MRT isn't just a win for your biceps and glutes—it's like therapy for your mind.

Exercise releases those feel-good endorphins, but MRT goes further by improving focus, boosting mood, and reducing stress levels faster than a reality TV contestant can cry during a heartfelt confession about their pet goldfish.

Plus, MRT sessions demand your full attention.

Between counting reps or tracking time, perfecting your form, and remembering to breathe, there's no room for overthinking that time you accidentally called your teacher 'Mum' in Year 4. It's an all-consuming, stress-relieving mental escape.

Why Time-Efficiency Matters

We're all busy. Whether you're juggling work, family, or just trying to squeeze in some me-time, finding hours to spend in the gym can feel impossible. MRT workouts pack a punch in as little as 20-30 minutes.

It's like a shot of espresso for your fitness goals—short, intense, and guaranteed to wake things up. But unlike those quick fixes that leave you unsatisfied, MRT leaves you feeling energised and accomplished.

Build Your First MRT Routine: Step-by-Step

Ready to jump in? Let's put together a simple MRT routine that'll have you sweating, smiling (eventually), and smashing those fitness goals.

Step 1: Pick Your Exercises

Choose 4-5 compound movements that work multiple muscle groups. Here's a starter list:

- **Squats or Lunges** (legs, core)
- **Push-Ups** (chest, shoulders, triceps)
- **Bent-Over Rows** (back, biceps)
- **Bridges** (glutes, hamstrings, core)

- **Plank with Shoulder Taps** (core, shoulders)

Step 2: Set Your Intervals
For beginners, try this:

- 30 seconds of work
- 15 seconds of rest
  Complete all exercises in a circuit, one after the other.

Step 3: Choose Your Total Time
Start with a manageable goal:

- **Beginner:** 10-15 minutes (2-3 rounds of your circuit)
- **Intermediate:** 20 minutes (4-5 rounds)
- **Advanced:** 25-30 minutes (as many rounds as you can handle without crying... too much)

Step 4: Adjust and Progress
As you get stronger, increase the work interval (e.g., 40 seconds on, 15 seconds off), add more rounds, or level up to heavier weights. MRT is all about progression—keep pushing your limits!

Step 5: Cool Down
After you've crushed your session, spend 5-10 minutes stretching. Trust me, your muscles will thank you, and it'll prevent you from walking like a robot the next day. Possibly.

Bottom Line
Metabolic Resistance Training isn't just a workout; it's a fast-track ticket to better health, a sharper mind, and an overall sense of accomplishment. Start small, build consistently, and remember: the only bad workout is the one you didn't do.

If you want some complete MRT workouts you can do anytime, anywhere, I've put together a collection of workout videos you can just push play on and follow along.

Just visit **www.anthonypunshon.com/rise-above-workouts** or scan the QR code below:

CHAPTER 14

Building Your Personal Fitness Routine

"Work it harder, make it better, do it faster, makes us stronger." - Daft Punk

When it comes to exercise, one size definitely does *not* fit all. You don't need some bland, cookie-cutter routine that feels about as exciting as reading the privacy policy of a toaster app. Instead, let's create a fitness plan that works for *you*—one that's flexible, fun, and doesn't make you want to fake a sudden leg injury.

Let's break down how to build your own fitness routine, combining the powerhouse combo of walking and Metabolic Resistance Training (MRT).

Step 1: Assess Your Starting Point
Before diving in headfirst, take a minute to think about where you're at. How active are you right now? Are you a sofa enthusiast, a weekend warrior, or someone who occasionally remembers they own a pair of trainers?

Wherever you're at, that's fine. This is just your starting point. We're not looking for perfection; we're looking for progress that doesn't make you want to throw in the towel halfway through.

Step 2: Set Your Goals
Let's keep this simple—what do you actually *want* out of this?

- **Mental clarity?** Walking can clear your head faster than your boss can send a 'quick question' email at 5pm on a Friday.
- **Strength and endurance?** MRT is your ticket to feeling like a superhero—minus the cape.
- **More energy, less stress, maybe drop a bit of weight?** The combo of walking and MRT will have you feeling better than an espresso shot to the soul.

Instead of "I want to get fit," try something specific like, "I want to feel less stressed and be able to carry my shopping bags without feeling like I'm wrestling a feisty badger with something to prove."

Step 3: Balance Your Routine
Here's where the magic mix of chill and challenge comes in. Walking brings the zen, and MRT brings the oomph.

Walking

- **How often?** 3-5 times a week.
- **How long?** Start with 20-30 minutes or split it into shorter strolls if that's more doable.
- **Bonus tip:** Walking after meals helps with digestion, keeps blood sugar steady, and gives you a perfectly good excuse to escape your phone's never-ending notifications.

MRT

- **How often?** 2-3 times a week.

- **How long?** A quick 20-30 minute session.
- **What to include:** Compound movements like squats, push-ups, and rows. If you're feeling fancy-pants, throw in some squat thrusts for an added challenge.

Step 4: Plan Your Week
Here's a simple, no-fuss template to get you started:

- **Monday:** MRT
- **Tuesday:** Walk
- **Wednesday:** Rest or light walk
- **Thursday:** MRT
- **Friday:** Walk
- **Saturday:** MRT
- **Sunday:** Long walk or rest

Tweak this to suit your schedule and energy levels. This isn't some hardcore drill sergeant routine—it's flexible, like yoga pants on a lazy Sunday.

Step 5: Make It Enjoyable
If your routine feels like a punishment, it won't last. So make it fun!

- Cue up your favourite podcast or playlist while you walk.
- Turn MRT sessions into mini-competitions with yourself—how many sumo squats can you smash out before you collapse? *(Disclaimer: Please don't actually collapse. Push yourself, but always work within your limits. No one's winning medals for overdoing it in their living room.)*
- Try new routes, new exercises, or add some social time by inviting a friend (or bribing them with coffee after).

This is about building a habit you *want* to keep—so add a little spice!

Bottom Line

Your fitness routine should work with your life, not against it. Start small, keep it consistent, and don't be afraid to change things up as you go. With walking and MRT in your corner, you're on the way to feeling stronger, healthier, and more balanced—one step, and one lift, at a time.

CHAPTER FIFTEEN

Tracking Progress Without Obsession

"Every step you take, every move you make, I'll be watching you." - The Police

When it comes to fitness, tracking progress is important. But let's be honest: it's easy to go from "I'm checking in to see how I'm doing" to "I'm refreshing my fitness app like it owes me money."

Obsessing over every pound, step, or rep can suck the joy out of things faster than a hoover at a biscuit factory.

In this chapter, we'll explore how to track progress in a way that keeps you motivated without making you feel like a prisoner to your goals.

Why Tracking Matters

First things first—tracking your progress isn't just about numbers. It's about recognising how far you've come. Maybe your trousers are a bit looser, or you're not wheezing like a punctured accordion after climbing a flight of stairs. Wins come in all shapes and sizes, and tracking helps you celebrate them.

The Dangers of Obsession

Here's the trap: when you become obsessed with metrics, you risk losing sight of what really matters—how you *feel*. You might have crushed your MRT session, but if the scale doesn't budge, it's easy to spiral into "Why bother?" territory.

Obsession turns tracking from a helpful tool into a joy-sucking black hole. Let's avoid that, shall we?

What to Track (and What to Ignore)

Let's focus on the stuff that really counts:

- **Strength Gains:** Can you lift more? Do more reps? Hold that plank for longer?
- **Stamina:** Can you walk further or faster without collapsing like a soggy cardboard box?
- **Mental Clarity:** Do you feel less stressed? More focused?
- **Mood Improvements:** Are you feeling happier or more energised?

Here's what to ignore:

- **Daily Weight Fluctuations:** Your weight can vary for a bajillion reasons. It doesn't define your progress.
- **Perfect Step Counts:** Close enough is good enough.
- **Comparisons to Others:** Your journey is yours. Don't let someone else's highlight reel mess with your mindset.

Tools That Keep You on Track

1. **Fitness Apps:** Use them for guidance, not gospel.
2. **Progress Photos:** A picture is worth a thousand words (or a thousand pushups).
3. **Strength and Endurance Milestones:** Keep a note of how much you can lift or how far you can walk. Seeing those numbers improve feels like winning a gold medal in the Olympics of You.

Bottom Line

Track your progress to celebrate how far you've come, not to punish yourself for how far you think you have to go. Remember, it's about progress, not perfection. Keep your focus on the journey and the small wins that stack up over time.

CHAPTER SIXTEEN

The Power of Consistency

"Ain't about how fast I get there, ain't about what's waiting on the other side. It's the climb." - Miley Cyrus

When it comes to fitness and mental well-being, consistency is the secret sauce. It's not the flashy one-off efforts that lead to lasting change; it's the small, steady steps that build momentum. Think of it as the tortoise and the hare situation, except this time the tortoise is rocking running shoes and a solid workout playlist.

Why Consistency Matters

Consistency might not sound glamorous, but it's the backbone of success in both fitness and life. Showing up regularly, even when you're not in the mood, is what separates those who achieve their goals from those who don't. It's like building a house—you don't lay all the bricks in one day, but over time, the structure takes shape.

In fitness, this means doing the work even when Netflix whispers sweet nothings like it's your long-lost lover. It's those regular workouts, daily walks, and mindful meal choices that add up to big results.

The Compound Effect

Ever heard of the compound effect? It's the idea that small, consistent actions, repeated over time, lead to significant improvements. Think of it like saving money. A few quid here and there might not seem like much, but over time, it adds up to a nice little nest egg—or at least enough for a last-minute trip to a beachside shack with questionable WiFi.

The same principle applies to your health. Every workout, every healthy meal, every extra step you take contributes to your overall progress. Alone, each effort might seem insignificant, but together they're a game-changer.

Practical Tips for Staying Consistent

1. Create a Routine
Block out time for your workouts like you're scheduling an important meeting with your boss—except this one involves fewer spreadsheets and more sweat. Bonus: No one's judging your workout gear, even if it's that Van Halen t-shirt you've had since 1982.

2. Start Small
Don't aim to become a fitness superhero overnight. Start with goals so manageable they make you chuckle. A 20-minute walk or a quick MRT session is your gateway to greatness—minus the dramatic rooftop pose.

3. Celebrate Small Wins
Did you manage to show up three times this week? That's a win! Treat yourself to something simple, like your favourite coffee or a

guilt-free binge of *The Great British Bake Off*. Celebrate without undoing all your hard work—looking at you, triple-chocolate cheesecake.

4. Find an Accountability Buddy
Preferably someone who won't let you bail with excuses like "The dog ate my trainers." Whether it's a friend or a fitness coach, having someone to share your wins (and hilarious workout fails) keeps you on track.

5. Track Your Progress
Use a journal or app to record your progress. Nothing feels better than seeing tangible proof that you're evolving from a sofa enthusiast to a walking, MRT-smashing legend. Just don't obsess over every minor fluctuation—save that energy for decoding your pet's mysterious behaviour.

Bottom Line
Consistency isn't about perfection; it's about persistence. It's showing up, doing the work, and trusting the process. The results might not come overnight, but with patience and commitment, they will come. So lace up those trainers, stick to your plan, and remember: it's the climb that makes you stronger.

CHAPTER SEVENTEEN

Rest and Recovery: Fitness's Secret Weapons

"You've got to know when to hold 'em, know when to fold 'em." - Kenny Rogers

We all love a good sweat session, right? But here's a plot twist: real progress doesn't just happen when you're busting out squats or smashing your MRT circuit. It happens when you're horizontal on the sofa, binge-watching *Is It Cake* with a smug sense of accomplishment.

Rest and recovery aren't just for wimps—they're for winners. Think of them as the backstage crew making sure your fitness show runs smoothly.

Why Rest and Recovery Matter

Picture your muscles as a group of toddlers at a birthday party. They're hyped, running around like maniacs, but if you don't give them a breather, things are going to get messy—cake on the walls, tears, and someone inevitably face-planting into the jelly.

Rest is your muscle's nap time. It helps them calm down, recover, and get ready to cause chaos another day.

Skipping rest is a one-way ticket to burnout city, complete with a side of injury and a deep hatred for anything involving stairs.

The Science of Recovery

Here's what really happens when you work out: your muscles get teeny tiny tears. (Don't panic, it's a good thing.) During rest, your body repairs these tears, building stronger, more resilient muscles. It's like upgrading your armour in a video game—level up, baby!

Now, if you skip rest, you're basically leaving your muscles stuck in noob mode. And nobody wants that.

Skipping rest is also like pulling a cake out of the oven too soon. Sure, it might look fine on the outside, but inside? Gooey chaos. Let it rest, and you'll get the perfect bake.

Practical Tips for Optimal Recovery

1. Prioritise Sleep

Sleep isn't just for beauty queens. It's when your body does its best work—repairing muscles, refreshing your mind, and erasing that awkward thing you said in that meeting earlier. Aim for 7-9 hours. And for the love of all things holy, stop doom-scrolling at midnight.

2. Active Recovery

Rest days don't mean turning into a human burrito. Light activities like walking, yoga, or chasing your dog around the garden keep you moving without turning your muscles into jelly.

3. Hydrate and Refuel

Think of water as your internal WD-40—it keeps everything running smoothly. And don't forget nutrient-packed foods to fuel your recovery. Pro tip: pizza with veggies totally counts. You know… in the appropriate amounts.

4. Foam Rolling and Stretching

Foam rollers: the gym world's version of a medieval torture device. Painful? Yes. Effective? Absolutely. Use them to ease muscle tension and keep things flexible. Just don't scream too loudly, or your neighbours might think you're wrestling a wild animal.

5 Listen to Your Body

Feeling more wiped out than a toddler after a sugar crash? Take an extra rest day. Your body's smarter than you think—it'll tell you what it needs, but only if you're willing to listen.

The Bottom Line

Rest days aren't for the lazy—they're for the smart. They're the secret weapon that turns all your hard work into actual progress. So kick back, relax, and let your body do its thing. Trust me, your muscles (and your knees) will thank you.

QUICK WINS

Your Cheat Sheet to a Fitter Body

Well done for making it through Part 2! Whether you're here to refresh your memory or skip straight to the action, this cheat sheet is your shortcut to all things fitness. Let's break it down into bite-sized pieces so you can hit the ground running—or walking, or lifting—whatever works for you.

Key Concepts Recap

- **Walking: Your Fitness Gateway Drug**
  Walking isn't just for getting to the corner shop; it's the unsung hero of physical and mental health. It boosts your mood, burns calories, and clears your mind faster than you can say "I need a break." Plus, it's free, and you already know how to do it.

- **Metabolic Resistance Training (MRT): Maximum Impact in Minimum Time**
  MRT is the Swiss Army knife of workouts: efficient, effective, and versatile. It's your one-stop shop for torching calories, building strength, and feeling like a superhero in training—cape optional.

- **Build a Routine That Fits Your Life**
  Forget trying to squeeze your square-peg schedule into a round-hole workout plan. Your fitness routine should work with your life, not against it. Whether you're a morning bird or a night owl, find what fits and stick to it.

- **Track Progress Without Turning into a Spreadsheet**
  Celebrate your wins without getting obsessed over the numbers. Your fitness journey isn't a stock ticker; it's more like a highlights reel. Focus on how you feel, what you can do, and the small victories that add up over time.

- **Rest and Recovery: The Secret Sauce**
  Rest days aren't for slackers; they're for smart cookies. Proper recovery prevents burnout and injuries while helping you come back stronger. So embrace the downtime—your muscles (and sanity) will thank you.

Action Steps

1. **Take a Walk**
   Set aside 20–30 minutes 3-5 times a week for a walk. Whether it's a gentle stroll or a power walk that leaves your neighbours wondering what you're late for, just get those steps in. Bonus points if you can hit a park or trail for some fresh air therapy.

2. **Start with MRT**

Choose 3–4 exercises (like squats, push-ups, and lunges) and do them in a circuit. Work for 30–60 seconds per exercise, rest for a minute, and repeat for 3–4 rounds. Quick, sweaty, and done before your excuses can catch up.

3. **Build Your Routine**
Decide how often you'll work out and stick to it. Maybe it's MRT three times a week with walks on your off days. The key is consistency—not perfection.

4. **Track Small Wins**
Keep a journal or app to note your progress. Lifted heavier weights? Managed more push-ups? Outpaced that smug jogger in the park? Write it down and celebrate.

5. **Embrace Rest Days**
Plan at least one rest day per week. Use it for light activity like yoga or stretching, or just binge that new show guilt-free. Remember, recovery is part of the process.

Final Pep Talk

You've got the tools to transform your fitness journey—one step, one lift, one rest day at a time. Remember, it's not about perfection but progress. So lace up, tune into your favourite pump-up track, and keep moving forward. The fitter, stronger, more confident version of you is just around the corner.

SUCCESS STORIES

Stronger Than Yesterday

How Kate Found Her Power, One Step at a Time

I've always been the type to just power through whatever life threw at me. People saw me as this strong, resilient woman. But after a few too many rough patches, I realised I needed help. Feeling constantly down and gaining weight from medication after therapy didn't quite do the trick, I knew something had to change.

The wake-up call came when I saw a picture of myself that I just couldn't stand. If I didn't want to see myself in photos, it was time to do something about it. Plus, I felt bloated all the time and just... off. So, I decided to take control of my diet and exercise.

Before this epiphany, my meals were all about convenience—anything quick and easy with big portions. But I made some big changes. I started controlling my portions better, made healthier food choices, cut down on carbs but kept the good ones, and discovered that food prep isn't as time-consuming as I thought. Oh, and I finally started drinking enough water, which made a huge difference.

Of course, it wasn't all smooth sailing. I learned not to beat myself up when things didn't go as planned. Even on bad days, I made sure not to resort to takeaways and reminded myself that one bad meal didn't ruin everything. As long as most of my meals were on point, I was doing great.

When it came to exercise, I found my groove with 30-minute MRT sessions that felt doable. Breaking workouts into small, manageable chunks and having some solid motivation kept me from giving up. I used to make excuses about not having time and would quit easily, but not anymore.

These days, I'm up early, working out four times a week. It makes me more productive and sets a positive tone for the day. I'm hitting my weight targets and feel less tired and more energised throughout my daily activities. Exercise has become such a natural part of my routine that it feels weird not to work out regularly.

And the mental health benefits? Huge. I'm more positive and handle daily challenges better. Getting up early and sticking to my routine gives me a sense of readiness and energy for the day. About four weeks in, I started noticing improvements in my mood, and seeing physical changes made me feel even more positive.

I've got more energy, sleep better, and don't feel sluggish in the mornings anymore. I'm proud of myself for making healthier choices even when eating out, which boosted my confidence and made me more content in my relationships.

My advice to anyone considering similar changes? Just go for it. The hardest step is the first one, but once you get your mind focused, long-lasting change is totally achievable. Having a supportive and motivational team behind you helps a lot too.

I also want to address a common misconception: while food might seem like a reward, its satisfaction is short-lived compared to the lasting benefits of a healthy lifestyle. Initially, I kept my changes quiet to avoid the shame of potential failure. But eventually, I found tremendous support from my husband and friends, who encouraged me to stick with my new habits.

Looking ahead, I plan to sustain these changes for the long term. Over ten weeks, I learned to enjoy "bad" foods in moderation without missing them much. When I do treat myself, it's in small amounts, and I quickly get back on track.

Reflecting on my journey, I highlight the importance of mental readiness and the realisation that I needed to work for change. The progress, though initially slow, came faster than expected, and the health benefits and improved self-esteem have been substantial rewards for my efforts.

Part 3: Nutrition

Eating Well Without Losing Your Mind

CHAPTER EIGHTEEN

Healthy Eating Without the Diet Drama

"A little bit of this, a little bit of that." - Fergie

Let's be real—when it comes to eating well, many of us immediately picture endless bowls of plain lettuce, joylessly poking at a sad cucumber slice while our taste buds weep. But healthy eating doesn't have to feel like you're auditioning for a reality show called *Salad and Sadness.*

In fact, eating well can be downright delicious, and yes, it's backed by science. The right nutrition fuels your body, sharpens your mind, and keeps your mood as balanced as a waiter carrying a pyramid of champagne flutes through a crowded dance floor.

The trick? It's all about making sustainable choices, not chasing the latest kale-infused trend you've seen on TikTok..

The Basics of Balance

Healthy eating is all about variety and moderation. Think of your plate like a party, and you're the host. You want a mix of guests:

- **Carbs** bring the energy, like the life of the party who never stops dancing.
- **Protein** is the reliable friend helping you move house (or rebuild your muscles).
- **Fats** are the chilled-out guests keeping everyone calm and in check.
- **Fibre** is your no-nonsense pal making sure the place doesn't get too messy (aka your digestion stays on track).

No single food is off-limits, but it's all about balance. Ate a doughnut for breakfast? That's fine—just don't make it an everyday thing, and balance it out with a nutrient-packed lunch.

Treats are part of life, but if your morning routine consistently resembles a bakery raid, it's time for a rethink.

Let's Talk About Snacks

Snacks often get a bad rap, but they can actually be the MVPs of your nutritional game. Think of them as your trusty sidekicks—always ready to swoop in and save you from the dreaded 3pm slump when your stomach's grumbling louder than Dave after losing the pub quiz.

In fact, science backs this up: eating smaller, more frequent meals or snacks can help keep your blood sugar steady, your energy levels up, and your hand out of the communal biscuit tin. The key is just not to turn "snacking" into "second breakfast, third lunch, and midnight feast."

Smart Snacks That Won't Betray You:

- **Protein-packed heroes** like Greek yoghurt, hard-boiled eggs, or a handful of nuts. These will keep you full and help you avoid the "hangry monster" stage.
- **Fibre-filled champions** like carrot sticks with hummus or an apple with peanut butter. They'll keep your digestion happy and leave you feeling smugly healthy.
- **Healthy fats** like avocado on whole-grain crackers—because who doesn't love a snack that feels fancy? If you want to eat them wearing a top hat and monocle, I won't judge.

And look, sometimes only chocolate will do. No judgement. Pair it with a handful of almonds or a cheeky banana slice so it's less of a guilty pleasure and more of a tactical morale boost.

Snacks are your allies, not your downfall—use them wisely, and they'll help keep you fuelled, focused, and feeling fabulous.

Practical Tips for Balanced Eating

1. Plan Ahead
Meal prep doesn't have to mean spending your Sunday cooking like you're feeding an army of fitness influencers. Just plan a few healthy meals or snacks to keep you on track.

2. The 80/20 Rule
Aim to eat nutrient-dense, whole foods 80% of the time, and save 20% for the fun stuff. Yes, this includes pizza and the occasional cheeky takeaway.

3. Hydrate Like a Champ
Often, thirst masquerades as hunger. Keep a water bottle handy and stay hydrated—it's a simple way to feel better overall.

4. Mindful Eating

Take time to enjoy your food. Sit down, chew slowly, and appreciate your meal. It's harder to enjoy a bag of crisps when you're inhaling it at your desk.

5. Portion Control
Serve your meals on smaller plates to trick your brain into thinking you're eating more. It's like Jedi mind tricks for your stomach.

Bottom Line
Healthy eating isn't about perfection or deprivation. It's about making choices that nourish your body and mind while still enjoying life. So, ditch the guilt, savour your meals, and remember—it's all about balance.

CHAPTER NINETEEN

Feed Your Brain: Nutrients for Mental Health

"Feed your head." - Jefferson Airplane

Let's set the scene: You're midway through the day, staring at your computer like it's a Magic 8-Ball that will somehow give you the answers to life's great questions. But instead of getting any clarity, your brain feels like it's running on dial-up, complete with a symphony of robotic screeches and blips that sounds like R2-D2 having a meltdown. Sound familiar?

Well, it turns out your brain might just be craving some top-tier fuel. And no, I'm not talking about your third cup of coffee or the emergency chocolate stash in your drawer (though we've all been there). I'm talking about nutrients—the VIPs of mental clarity and mood stability.

The Brain-Food Connection: It's Science, Not Sorcery

Your brain is like a high-performance engine. Sure, it'll run on fumes for a while, but if you want it firing on all cylinders, you need premium fuel.

Enter omega-3s, B-vitamins, and magnesium—the holy trinity of brain nourishment.

Omega-3s are like the trusty mechanics of your brain, keeping everything running smoothly. Found in fatty fish like salmon and mackerel, these essential fats reduce inflammation and improve communication between brain cells. Basically, they're the ultimate brain whisperers.

B-vitamins, on the other hand, are your brain's hype squad. They help with energy production and neurotransmitter regulation, which means they play a big role in keeping your mood on an even keel. Think of them as the personal assistants who ensure your brain never misses a meeting or forgets a name at a party.

And then there's magnesium—the unsung hero of mental health. This mineral is like a calming hug for your nervous system. Feeling stressed? Magnesium steps in like a bouncer, gently escorting tension out the door.

Why Are These Nutrients So Important?

Picture your brain as the star performer in a one-man show. Without the right support, even the best actors can crumble. These nutrients are the backstage crew, making sure everything's in place so your brain can deliver an Oscar-worthy performance.

Studies have shown that a diet rich in omega-3s, B-vitamins, and magnesium can reduce symptoms of depression, improve memory, and even help you stay sharp as you age. In other words, feeding your brain isn't just about surviving the day—it's about thriving in the long run.

Practical Steps: How to Get These Nutrients Without Becoming a Health Guru

1. Omega-3s: Fish and Beyond
If you love fish, fantastic—aim for two servings of fatty fish per week. Not a fan? No worries. Walnuts, flaxseeds, and chia seeds are excellent plant-based sources. And if you're thinking, "Yeah, but will I actually eat those?" there's always omega-3 supplements. Just don't try to sneak fish oil into your morning coffee.

2. B-Vitamins: More Than Just Boring Broccoli
You'll find B-vitamins in whole grains, leafy greens, eggs, and dairy. If breakfast usually involves grabbing a croissant on the go, consider swapping it for a bowl of fortified cereal or a quick veggie omelette. Fancy-pants without the fancy effort.

3. Magnesium: The Chill Pill You Can Eat
Nuts, seeds, and dark chocolate are your magnesium go-tos. Yes, you read that right—chocolate can help you relax. So, the next time someone questions your snacking choices, just smile knowingly and say, "It's for my mental health."

Action Step: Your Brain-Boosting Challenge
This week, try adding one brain-boosting food to your daily meals. Maybe it's a handful of walnuts in your yoghurt, a side of spinach with dinner, or a square (or two) of dark chocolate. See how it feels to give your brain the five-star treatment it deserves.

Bottom Line
Your brain is a big deal—it's the control centre of everything you do, from solving complex problems to remembering where you left your keys. By feeding it the nutrients it craves, you're not just supporting your mental health; you're setting yourself up for a sharper, brighter, and more balanced life.

So, grab some fish, sprinkle those seeds, and embrace the magic of brain-friendly eating. Trust me, your future self—the one crushing deadlines and remembering everyone's birthday—will thank you.

CHAPTER TWENTY

Protein—Your Body's Unsung Hero

"Work it harder, make it better, do it faster, makes us stronger." - Daft Punk

As far as nutrients go, protein is the perfectionist who can't just do the bare minimum. Protein is out here writing its own CV while carbs and fats are napping on the job.

You've probably heard it touted as the building block of muscles, but its résumé doesn't stop there. Protein is also crucial for your mental health, helping to keep you sharp, focused, and resilient.

Why Protein Matters
Protein isn't just about getting ripped or recovering after workouts (though it's great for that). It's vital for repairing tissues, producing enzymes, and keeping your immune system in fighting shape. But the unsung hero here? Its role in mental health.

Protein helps regulate neurotransmitters like serotonin and dopamine—the very chemicals that keep your mood stable and your brain firing on all cylinders. Skimp on protein, and you might feel sluggish, unfocused, and ready to bite someone's head off over minor inconveniences, like realising you've run out of toilet paper mid-sit.

How Much Do You Actually Need?

Forget the one-size-fits-all approach. The amount of protein you need depends on your age, activity level, and goals. As a rule of thumb, aim for 1.2–2.0 grams of protein per kilogram of body weight. Translation: if you weigh 70 kg, you're looking at 84–140 grams of protein daily.

Top Protein Sources

Here's where it gets exciting (and tasty). Protein doesn't have to mean bland chicken breast and boiled eggs forever. You've got options:

- **Lean meats and poultry** like chicken, turkey, and lean cuts of beef.
- **Fish and seafood** such as salmon, tuna, and prawns are not only protein-packed but also loaded with brain-boosting omega-3s.
- **Plant-based proteins** like lentils, chickpeas, tofu, and tempeh if you're keeping it veggie.
- **Dairy and eggs** with Greek yoghurt, cottage cheese, and good old eggs being protein powerhouses.
- **Protein powders** for a quick, convenient boost when you're short on time or can't face another boiled egg.

How to Incorporate Protein Without Feeling Like You're Training for Mr. Universe

1. Lean Meats and Poultry

Think chicken breast, turkey, or a cheeky bit of steak. These guys are like the main characters of the protein world—reliable, effective, and they don't need a flashy marinade to get the job done. But hey, throw in some seasoning if you want to feel fancy.

2. Eggs
Nature's pre-packaged protein bombs. Whether you scramble, poach, or go full MasterChef with an omelette, eggs have your back. Bonus points for making them look Instagram-worthy with a side of avocado.

3. Greek Yoghurt
Thick, creamy, and packed with protein. It's like dessert, but without the sugar coma. Add some berries and a drizzle of honey, and suddenly you're the kind of person who "does brunch."

4. Legumes and Lentils
Beans, chickpeas, lentils—they're the unsung heroes of the protein world. They might not have the star power of steak, but they're like that dependable friend who always shows up with coffee after a long night—without being asked. Plus, they're budget-friendly and won't side-eye you for being cheap.

5. Protein Shakes
Quick, easy, and makes you feel like you're in a montage scene from a fitness ad. Just don't be that person shaking up a storm in the middle of a quiet office—no one needs to hear your blender bottle auditioning for a drum solo.

6. Tofu and Tempeh
For the plant-based crew, these are your go-to options. Think of them as blank canvases waiting for your culinary genius to transform them. Marinate them, fry them, or toss them in a stir-fry—they'll soak up flavours like a sponge.

7. Snacks on the Go

Protein bars, jerky, or a handful of nuts. Perfect for when you're out and about, pretending you've got your life together. Just be mindful of those sneaky sugar bombs masquerading as "healthy" snacks.

Action Steps

- Take stock of your current protein intake. Are you hitting the recommended amount? If not, start by adding a high-protein snack or upgrading your breakfast.
- Plan at least one meal a day that focuses on protein. It could be as simple as swapping out your usual sandwich for a chicken salad or adding a side of lentils to your dinner.
- Experiment with different protein sources to keep things interesting.

Bottom Line

Protein is your body and mind's best mate. It keeps you strong, sharp, and ready to tackle whatever life throws your way (even if it's another one of Janet's emails). Prioritise it, mix it up, and watch as your energy, focus, and mood get a serious upgrade.

CHAPTER TWENTY-ONE

Healthy Fats Without the Hype

"I need you, like water, like breath, like rain." - LeAnn Rimes

Let's talk about fats, the nutrient with a PR problem. For decades, they've been blamed for everything from heart disease to not fitting into your jeans after Christmas. But fats aren't the enemy—they're essential for your body to function properly and for you to feel your best. In fact, they're like the quiet hero of your diet, saving the day while carbs and protein hog the spotlight.

What Are Healthy Fats, and Why Do You Need Them?
Let's break it down: healthy fats are the VIPs of the nutrient world. They support brain function, boost your mood, and help your body absorb vitamins like A, D, E, and K—think of them as the slick operators making sure your internal systems run like clockwork.

Here's a quick look at the major players:

- **Monounsaturated fats**: Found in avocados, olive oil, and nuts, these fats help lower bad cholesterol and keep your heart happy.
- **Polyunsaturated fats**: Omega-3s and omega-6s fall under this category. They're the brain-boosters, helping to reduce inflammation and support mental health. You'll find them in fatty fish, flaxseeds, and walnuts.
- **Saturated fats**: These get a mixed review. A little bit is fine (butter, coconut oil), but too much can still give your arteries a tough time. Moderation is key.

Fats and Mental Health: A Love Story

Here's where it gets juicy—healthy fats can do wonders for your brain. Studies have shown that omega-3s, in particular, are linked to lower levels of depression and anxiety. They help build cell membranes in your brain, improving communication between neurons. Think of them as the social butterflies of your nervous system, making sure everyone's getting along.

Busting the Myths

Myth 1: Eating Fat Makes You Fat

Not true. It's all about calories in vs. calories out. Healthy fats are more calorie-dense, sure, but they're also more satisfying. Ever notice how a handful of almonds keeps you full longer than a low-fat cereal bar? That's the magic of fats.

Myth 2: All Fats Are Created Equal

Also false. There's a world of difference between the fats in an avocado and those in a packet of crisps. One supports your health; the other makes your taste buds happy for approximately 3.7 seconds before leading you down a path of regret.

How Much Fat Do You Actually Need?

The NHS recommends that about 30% of your daily calories come from fats, with no more than 10% from saturated fats. For most people, that's around 70 grams of fat per day, depending on your calorie intake.

But a word of caution, though. Fats are calorie-dense at over twice the calories per gram of protein and carbs, they can quietly push your daily intake through the roof faster than you can scroll past your ex's holiday photos on social media if you're not careful. That doesn't mean you should avoid them, just be mindful. A little fat goes a long way, and balance is everything. You don't need to eat half a jar of peanut butter to reap the benefits—though I get it, we've all been there.

How to Incorporate Healthy Fats Without Going Overboard

1. Go Nuts
Almonds, walnuts, pistachios—take your pick. They're easy to snack on and packed with monounsaturated fats. Just watch your portion sizes; it's easy to turn "healthy" into "how did I eat the entire bag?"

2. Avocado Everything
Spread it on toast, blend it into smoothies, or just eat it with a spoon. Avocados are versatile and delicious, proving once again that fats can be both functional and fancy-pants. Man-bun and food-filled Insta-grid optional.

3. Fish It Up
Salmon, mackerel, sardines—these are your go-to sources for omega-3s. Aim for at least two servings of fatty fish a week, and you'll be feeding your brain the good stuff.

4. Dress It Right
Swap your low-fat salad dressings (often loaded with sugar) for olive oil and balsamic vinegar. Your taste buds and your heart will thank you.

5. Cook Smart
Use oils like olive, coconut, or avocado for cooking. Butter's fine too—in moderation. Remember, we're going for balance, not perfection.

Action Step: Fat-ify Your Next Meal
Pick one of the above strategies and add some healthy fats to your next meal. It's a simple, delicious way to boost your nutrition without turning your kitchen into a science experiment.

Bottom Line
Healthy fats are your brain's best friend and your body's secret weapon. Embrace them in moderation, and you'll feel the difference in your energy, mood, and overall well-being. So grab that olive oil, channel your inner Gordon Ramsey, and start cooking up a storm. Just leave the deep-fried Mars bars for the occasional trip down memory lane.

CHAPTER TWENTY-TWO

The Fibre Fix: Gut Health and Mental Clarity

"Shake it like a Polaroid picture." - OutKast

Let's face it, fibre isn't exactly the rock star of the nutrient world. It's more like the quiet, dependable band member who keeps the group from falling apart. But don't be fooled—this understated hero is crucial for both physical and mental well-being. In fact, fibre might just be the unsung champion of your health journey.

What Is Fibre, and Why Should You Care?
Fibre is a type of carbohydrate that your body can't digest, but don't let that fool you into thinking it's useless. Think of it as your digestive system's personal trainer, keeping things moving smoothly while cheering on your gut microbes.

There are two types:

- **Soluble fibre**: Think oatmeal and apples. It dissolves in water, forming a gel-like substance that helps lower cholesterol and stabilise blood sugar.
- **Insoluble fibre**: The gritty stuff in whole grains and vegetables that adds bulk to your stool and keeps things moving. Yes, we're talking about poop, and you'll thank fibre for making that a smoother experience.

Fibre's Secret Superpower: Mental Health

Here's where it gets interesting. Beyond its obvious physical benefits, fibre plays a surprising role in mental health. Studies have shown that a high-fibre diet can help reduce symptoms of anxiety and depression. Why? Because fibre feeds your gut bacteria, and a happy gut equals a happy mind. It's like giving your gut a group hug every time you eat a bowl of lentil soup.

How Much Fibre Do You Need?

The NHS recommends adults aim for about 30 grams of fibre a day. To put that in perspective, that's roughly:

- 1 slice of whole-grain bread
- 1 cup of broccoli
- 1 apple with the skin on
- And a decent handful of nuts

But here's the thing—most people barely hit 15 grams. So, if your current fibre intake wouldn't even impress a toddler, it's time to level up.

How to Get More Fibre Without Feeling Like You're Chewing on Cardboard

1. Sneak It In

Sprinkle flaxseeds or chia seeds on your morning cereal. Add an extra handful of spinach to your pasta sauce. Fibre can be stealthy like a ninja, but with less face paint.

2. Swap It Out
Switch white bread, rice, and pasta for their whole-grain cousins. It's like trading in your tired old sedan for a turbo-charged SUV. It might take a bit of getting used to, but once you do, you won't look back.

3. Snack Smart
Trade crisps and chocolate bars for raw veggies and hummus or a handful of almonds. Sure, they're not as glamorous, but they'll keep you full and happy longer.

4. Go Legumes
Beans, lentils, and chickpeas aren't just for vegetarians. Toss them in salads, soups, or stews, and watch your fibre intake soar. Bonus: They're cheap and versatile, so your wallet will thank you too.

5. Fibre Supplements
If all else fails, a supplement can help bridge the gap. Just remember, no supplement can replace a balanced diet, so don't let those orange gummies become your crutch.

Action Step: Fibre Up Your Next Meal
Today, pick one meal and make it a fibre powerhouse. Add beans to your salad, swap white rice for quinoa, or snack on an apple with almond butter. Your gut will be high-fiving you by bedtime.

Bottom Line
Fibre might not be flashy, but it's a game-changer for both your body and your mind. Embrace it, and you'll be fuelling your gut for a healthier, happier you. Now, get out there and fibre-up—you've got this!

CHAPTER TWENTY-THREE

Hydration Station: Water's Role in Mind and Body

"I'm dying of thirst but I'm drowning in the fountain." - Better Than Ezra

Picture this: It's mid-afternoon, and you're dragging yourself through the day. Your focus is shot, your energy's tanking, and you're debating whether to caffeinate or nap your way out of it. Before you do either, ask yourself: When was the last time I had a proper drink of water?

If the answer is "Does coffee count?" then congratulations—you've joined the ranks of the chronically dehydrated.

Why Hydration Matters
Water is the unsung hero of health—like that one friend who magically produces a spare phone charger when yours dies. Every cell in your body is basically calling out for water all day long. It's

the ultimate multitasker, delivering nutrients, flushing out toxins, and keeping everything running smoothly without so much as a pat on the back.

Let's break it down:

- **Brain Boost**: Even mild dehydration can mess with your mood, memory, and focus. Think of your brain as a sponge—when it's well-hydrated, it's plump and ready to absorb all the info. When it's parched, you're running on mental fumes.
- **Energy Levels**: Water is like fuel for your engine. Without it, you're as sluggish as a snail stuck in treacle.
- **Detox Duty**: Your kidneys love water. It helps them flush out waste and keep your system squeaky clean. Skimp on hydration, and your body struggles to do its job efficiently.

How to Tell You're Dehydrated

Dehydration can sneak up on you like a bad haircut—one minute you're fine, the next you're wondering how you got here. Here are the telltale signs:

- **Dry mouth**
- **Dark urine** (think less lemonade, more apple juice)
- **Fatigue**
- **Headaches**
- **Crankiness** (because no one's their best self when parched)

Making Water Exciting (Yes, Really)

Let's be honest: water can feel a bit, well, boring. But it doesn't have to be. Here's how to jazz it up:

1. **Infusions**: Add slices of cucumber, lemon, or a handful of mint. You'll feel fancy, like you're at a spa, even if you're just on the sofa binge-watching crime dramas.

2. **Sparkling Water**: If you miss the fizz of soda, sparkling water is your friend. Throw in some berries or a splash of juice for a treat.
3. **Herbal Teas**: They count towards your water intake and come in flavours like peppermint, chamomile, or fruity blends that feel like a warm hug.
4. **Water Apps**: Yes, there are apps to remind you to drink water. It's like having a hydration coach in your pocket.

Action Step: Hydration Challenge

For the next week, aim to down at least 8 glasses of water a day. If that sounds like a one-way ticket to spending your life in the loo, start small. Swap one sugary drink for water or set a reminder to sip throughout the day. By day three, you'll be feeling more energised, less foggy, and smug enough to start giving unsolicited hydration advice to your mates.

Bottom Line

Water is life. Literally. Staying hydrated gives your body and brain the juice they need to stop running on fumes. So grab that glass, fill it up, and give yourself a classy little toast. Bonus points if you air-clink and declare, "To not feeling like a dried-out houseplant!" Cheers!

CHAPTER TWENTY-FOUR

Practical Meal Planning Without the Hassle

"I'll be there for you (When the rain starts to pour)." - The Rembrandts

Let's face it: meal planning can feel about as appealing as a root canal. You know you should do it, but the thought of spreadsheets, calorie counts, and endless chopping is enough to make you want to curl up under a blanket fort with a takeaway menu and a faint sense of doom.

But here's the thing—meal planning doesn't have to be a soul-crushing chore. Done right, it's less about becoming a kitchen tyrant and more about setting yourself up for success without sacrificing all your free time.

So, how do we make meal planning easy, effective, and maybe even fun? Let's dive in.

The Science of Simplicity
Meal planning isn't just a way to save time; it's a tool for better nutrition, portion control, and keeping your stress levels in check. Studies show that people who plan their meals tend to eat more nutrient-dense foods and fewer processed snacks. Plus, there's the added bonus of saving money and reducing food waste—because, let's be honest, nobody needs another soggy bag of lettuce wilting away in the fridge.

But it's not just about the physical benefits. Knowing what's on the menu each day frees up mental space, cutting down on decision fatigue—the sneaky culprit behind bad choices.

After a long day, your brain's running on fumes, and suddenly the leftover cake is singing your name like it's auditioning for *The Voice*. Even pre-rebrand Mark Zuckerberg wore the same blue t-shirt and jeans every day just to avoid the morning "what-to-wear" dilemma. If a billionaire tech genius can skip wardrobe choices, you can skip dinner debates.

No more frantic post-work supermarket dashes or staring blankly into the fridge like it holds the secrets of the universe. That mental clarity? Absolutely priceless.

The Three Pillars of Hassle-Free Meal Planning
Let's break it down into three simple steps:

1. Plan Smart, Not Hard
Start with meals you already know and love. Have a go-to chicken stir-fry or a pasta dish that's both delicious and quick? Put those on repeat. Variety is great, but not if it sends you down a Pinterest rabbit hole.

Think of it like curating a playlist: stick to the hits, and sprinkle in a new recipe now and then for some spice.

2. Batch Cook Like a Boss

Batch cooking is your best mate. Whip up a big pot of chilli, soup, or a tray of roasted veggies on Sunday, and you've got a head start on the week. Freeze portions, mix and match, and suddenly, weekday meals become a game of delicious Tetris.

It's like meal planning's version of playing with Lego—except at the end, you get to eat your creations.

3. Prep Snacks to Avoid the "Hanger" Gremlin
When hunger strikes, you're either reaching for a healthy snack or tearing through a packet of biscuits like a caffeinated badger. Avoid the latter by prepping snacks in advance. Cut-up veggies, hummus, boiled eggs, or a handful of nuts—whatever keeps you from morphing into the "Hanger" Hulk.

Practical Meal Planning Hacks
Here's how to turn meal planning into a smoother ride, with fewer bumps and detours:

- **Theme Nights**: Designate each night with a theme to simplify choices. Taco Tuesday, Pasta Friday, or Stir-fry Saturday doesn't just make life easier—it gives you something to look forward to. Plus, it's a sneaky way to add variety without overthinking it. Bonus points if you rename Wednesday "Whatever's Left Night" to polish off those leftovers.

- **Love Your Leftovers**: Don't just tolerate leftovers—celebrate them! Yesterday's roast chicken can be today's salad star or the hero of a hearty sandwich. Leftovers save time, reduce waste, and make you feel like a culinary mastermind.

- **Shop with a List**: Think of your list as a supermarket survival guide. No more wandering aimlessly or impulse-buying a lifetime supply of chocolate biscuits. Stick to what you need, and your wallet—and waistline—will thank you.

- **Use a Meal Planning App**: These digital lifesavers help you store recipes, plan meals, and generate shopping lists. It's like having a personal assistant dedicated to your kitchen adventures, minus the salary.

- **The Freezer is Your Friend**: Batch-cooked meals, chopped veggies, and even smoothie bags can live happily in your freezer. It's like meal planning insurance for those days when cooking feels as appealing as a group chat with your entire extended family.

- **Prep Snacks Like a Pro**: Have healthy options at the ready to fend off the 3pm munchies. Carrot sticks, pre-portioned trail mix, or yoghurt pots can keep you from making questionable snack decisions, like that half-eaten pack of crisps lurking in the back of your cupboard.

Example Meal Plan: A Week of Simplicity

Here's a peek at what a week of balanced, no-hassle meals might look like:

Monday

Breakfast:	Overnight oats with berries (Prepped on Sunday night)
Lunch:	Leftover chilli from Sunday, served over brown rice (Batch cooked)
Dinner:	Stir-fried chicken and veggies with soy sauce (Quick, easy, and uses up leftover veg)
Snacks:	Apple slices with peanut butter, a handful of almonds

Tuesday

Breakfast:	Scrambled eggs with spinach and whole-grain toast (5-minute wonder)
Lunch:	Chicken salad wrap (Using leftover stir-fried chicken)
Dinner:	Tacos with black beans, salsa, and avocado (It's Taco Tuesday, after all)
Snacks:	Greek yoghurt with honey, boiled egg

Wednesday

Breakfast:	Smoothie (Prepped in a freezer bag, just blend and go)
Lunch:	Leftover tacos in a salad bowl format
Dinner:	Baked salmon with roasted sweet potatoes and broccoli (Minimal prep, maximum flavour)
Snacks:	Veggie sticks with hummus, handful of trail mix

Thursday

Breakfast:	Avocado toast with a sprinkle of chilli flakes
Lunch:	Leftover salmon and sweet potato salad
Dinner:	One-pot pasta with tomato, spinach, and lean sausage (Throw it all in and let it do its thing)
Snacks:	Cottage cheese with pineapple, a banana

Friday

Breakfast: Greek yoghurt with granola and mixed berries

Lunch: Leftover pasta from Thursday

Dinner: Homemade pizza using whole-grain base and your favourite toppings (Fun and customisable)

Snacks: Rice cakes with almond butter, a protein bar

Saturday

Breakfast: Pancakes made with oats and banana, topped with a dollop of Greek yoghurt

Lunch: DIY sandwich platter (Think picnic vibes)

Dinner: Grilled chicken kebabs with quinoa salad (Great for a weekend BBQ)

Snacks: Sliced veggies with tzatziki, handful of cashews

Sunday

Breakfast: Veggie-packed omelette (Great for using up odds and ends)

Lunch: Sunday roast or a hearty soup (Batch cook for leftovers)

Dinner: Light salad or leftovers from lunch

Snacks: Dark chocolate square or two, a piece of fruit

What We Did Here:

- **Batch Cooking**: Prepped chilli and roasted veggies on Sunday for the week ahead.
- **Leftovers**: Incorporated leftover proteins and veg into salads and wraps.
- **Theme Nights**: Taco Tuesday and Pizza Friday kept things simple and fun.
- **Prep Ahead**: Overnight oats, smoothie packs, and pre-chopped veggies saved time.
- **Versatility**: Snacks like Greek yoghurt and hummus fit seamlessly into multiple days.

Note: Your meal plan doesn't have to look this varied or involved. It could be as simple as rotating a few favourites each week. This example shows how easy it is to mix things up without adding extra work. Minimal effort, maximum payoff.

Action Step: Try a One-Week Meal Plan

For the next week, plan out your meals in advance. Start simple—maybe breakfast and lunch if planning all three feels overwhelming. Use the tips above, and don't forget to include snacks.

Take notes on what worked, what didn't, and tweak for the following week. Soon, you'll be a meal-planning wizard, conjuring up healthy, stress-free meals like it's second nature.

Bottom Line

Meal planning doesn't have to be a grind. With a few simple strategies, it can save you time, money, and mental energy—while keeping your nutrition on point. Embrace the process, experiment with what works for you, and remember: the goal isn't perfection, it's progress.

Now, get out there and plan your way to stress-free, balanced meals. Because life's too short to live on takeaway chips and regret.

QUICK WINS

Your Cheat Sheet to Guilt-Free Eating

You've made it through Part 3! As always, whether you're here to refresh your memory or skip straight to the practical bits, this cheat sheet will help you eat smarter without the stress. Let's dive in and make healthy eating as straightforward as your mum's Sunday roast.

Key Concepts Recap

Balanced Eating: The Goldilocks Approach
Not too much, not too little—just right. Balanced eating isn't about deprivation; it's about finding the sweet spot where your body and mind thrive. Think nutrient-dense meals with room for the odd treat. Yes, even that chocolate bar.

Nutrients for Mental Health: Feed Your Brain, Not Just Your Belly

Omega-3s, B-vitamins, magnesium—they're not just fancy words for the back of a supplement bottle. These are the VIPs of your mental health support squad. Incorporate them, and your brain will be doing cartwheels (or at least less sulking in a corner).

Protein: The Overachiever of the Nutrition World
Protein builds muscle, keeps you full, and stabilises blood sugar. It's like that kid in school who aced every subject and still found time to volunteer. Make it a regular guest at every meal.

Fats: The Misunderstood Bestie
Healthy fats are essential for brain function, hormone balance, and keeping your skin glowing like a Love Island contestant. Avocados, nuts, and olive oil are your new best friends—just don't invite them all to the party at once unless you're ready for a calorie explosion.

Fibre: The Unsung Hero
Fibre keeps your gut happy and your mind clear. It's like that backstage crew member who ensures the whole production runs smoothly. Load up on veggies, fruits, and whole grains, and let fibre work its magic.

Hydration: The Overlooked Champion
Water is life. Literally. Staying hydrated keeps your energy up, your mind sharp, and your body functioning like a well-oiled machine. Add a slice of lemon or a sprig of mint if plain water feels like a chore.

Action Steps

Plan Ahead Like a Kitchen Ninja
Take 10–15 minutes each week to plan your meals. Batch cook your favourites and keep healthy snacks within arm's reach. This way, when hunger strikes, you won't find yourself elbow-deep in a packet of biscuits.

Make Water Your BFF
Carry a water bottle wherever you go. Aim for 8 glasses a day, and jazz it up with infusions if plain water isn't your vibe. Remember, dehydration turns you into a grumpy raisin.

Build Balanced Plates
Each meal should be a mix of protein, healthy fats, and fibre. Think grilled chicken with roasted veg and quinoa, or scrambled eggs on whole-grain toast with a side of avocado. Fancy-pants meals optional.

Snack Smart
When hunger hits between meals, go for snacks like Greek yoghurt with berries or a handful of nuts. They'll keep you satisfied without wrecking your calorie count.

Tune Into Your Body
Listen to your hunger and fullness cues. You're not a human dustbin—stop eating when you're satisfied, not when the plate's clean. And yes, you can save the rest for later.

Final Pep Talk
Congratulations, you're now armed with the knowledge to conquer your nutrition game. Remember, healthy eating isn't about rigid rules or perfection. It's about finding what works for you and enjoying the journey—because life's too short to stress over a slice of cake.

So, grab your shopping list, plan those meals, and keep it simple, sustainable, and delicious. You've got this!

SUCCESS STORIES

From Mocha Overload to Morning Miles

How Claire Transformed Her Energy, Health, and Life—One Step at a Time

I grew up as one of those naturally sporty kids who seemed to stay fit and slim without even trying. A combination of balanced meals, correct portion sizes, regular sport, and a bit of good genetics kept me active and healthy throughout my childhood and teens. In my late teens and early twenties, I had a physically active job, and my social circle was filled with like-minded friends, so I carried on living a relatively healthy lifestyle. But mental health has always been a challenge for me. I was diagnosed with OCD in my teens and have tried countless anxiety medications over the years. Even so, exercise has always been my secret weapon for managing my mental health.

As I moved through my 30s, my health and appearance fluctuated. Sometimes I was too thin; other times, I'd let socialising take over and found myself a bit chubby. Having been diagnosed with endometriosis and adenomyosis, I knew staying at a healthy weight was essential for managing symptoms, but the severe fatigue that comes with these conditions often held me back. Then I became a mum, and everything changed. I felt the best I had in years, spending most of my time walking and no longer eating just for pleasure. But when I started my first full-time desk job in my late 30s, things took a turn. The lack of movement, countless mochas, and far too many biscuits left me feeling "yucky." My clothes were tight, I was constantly tired, and my mood swings were taking a toll at home. Something had to change.

I'd always known exercise made me feel better, but I kept telling myself I didn't have the time. I tried walking on my lunch breaks, which helped initially, but workload always got in the way. I realised I needed something more structured—something I couldn't ignore or put off. Alongside that, my diet needed an overhaul. I'd been eating whatever I wanted for years, thinking I could "get away with it." But age and a more sedentary lifestyle were starting to catch up with me. The first thing I changed was swapping my fully loaded mochas (three a day!) for a hot chocolate and black coffee combo. It sounds small, but it was transformative. Two years later, I don't even like the taste of my old mochas anymore. It's funny how your taste buds can adapt.

I also stopped grazing on cakes and biscuits at work, choosing to pack my own lunches instead. Leftovers or a ham wrap became my go-to, with a small chocolate bar for my sweet tooth. Portion control was another big shift. The first time I weighed out a portion of rice, I couldn't believe how little I was supposed to have. But over time, smaller portions felt natural, and I physically couldn't eat the amounts I used to. I stick to healthy eating during the week, allow myself a cheat day on Saturdays (because pizza is sacred), and focus on consistency and moderation.

The impact of these changes was almost immediate. Drinking more water left me feeling "cleansed," and cutting back on stodgy foods like bread helped me avoid that sluggish, weighed-down feeling—except for pizza on cheat day, of course! On tough days,

I'd remind myself how good I felt when I stuck to my plan and forced myself to get moving. Once I got up and started, I was in the zone and focused on the end result: feeling like myself again.

Exercise became another game-changer. I started with 30- to 45-minute low-impact classes focusing on strength and flexibility, which were manageable but effective. Walking has always been part of my routine, but I added more. Now, I walk the two miles to school in the mornings when I do drop-offs. Not only does it get me moving, but it also gives me extra time to chat with my son—a win-win. I aim for three classes a week, daily walks, and a longer family trek on Sundays. Even a small amount of movement releases those happy hormones and lifts my mood almost instantly.

The results weren't immediate—oh, how I wish they were—but the mood boost after exercising was undeniable. Over time, the physical changes followed. I've lost inches from my hips and waist, and I feel fitter, stronger, and more energised. My increased energy has transformed my daily life. Saturday mornings now start with a circuit class, followed by a full-on spring clean of the house. I'm more engaged with my son, able to bend down and play with him easily, and our Sunday walks have become a cherished family tradition. Even my husband has noticed the difference—he now hides the sweet jar for me because he knows I can't resist!

Work has benefited too. Walking to school instead of driving means no more sitting in traffic, and by the time I get to my desk with my black mocha, I'm energised and ready to tackle the day. The thought of feeling sluggish and tired is motivation enough to keep going. If I have a setback, I don't dwell on it. I start again because I know how much worse I feel when I don't move.

If you're thinking about making changes, my advice is to start small. Make one adjustment and notice how good it makes you feel, then build from there. Use an app to track your food—it's quick, easy, and helps you learn what works for you. Don't forget to allow yourself a cheat day, and if you miss a workout or slip up with your eating, don't beat yourself up. Just reset and keep going. Consistency is key.

Diet and exercise won't necessarily fix everything, especially if you're dealing with a mental health condition like I am. But they make a WORLD of difference. For me, exercise supports my medication and gives me a release I can't get elsewhere. I'll never forget the first time my son had a sugar rush—he was two years old, running around a restaurant, arms flailing, shouting "RAAAAH!" at the top of his lungs. That's how I imagine exercise works for adults—it lets us release all that pent-up energy and stress instead of keeping it bottled up.

Now, fitness and healthy eating are just part of my lifestyle. It doesn't feel like a programme or a chore—it's how I live. My support network has played a huge role in this. My boss encouraged me to prioritise fitness, even if it meant being late to work. My husband and son have been amazing, helping to eliminate temptations and making this a family journey. The friends I've made through fitness keep me motivated, and challenges tap into my competitive streak.

Looking back, the biggest driver was wanting to change and understanding how those changes would impact my life for the better. I don't plan on going backwards anytime soon—in fact, I'm already dreaming up my next walking challenge. The bug is back, and I'm loving it.

CONCLUSION

Soaring Higher: Your Rise Above Toolkit

And here we are, at the finish line. You've read through all the chapters, taken in the tips, and, hopefully, laughed at least once (even if it was just at my ridiculous analogies). You're now armed with a blueprint to rise above life's challenges, whether it's conquering your inner critic, smashing out a killer workout, or figuring out what on earth to cook for dinner.

But this isn't the end. It's the beginning of YOUR next chapter.

The Big Picture
Throughout this book, we've covered the trifecta of well-being: mindset, movement, and nutrition. Think of them as the Avengers of your health journey. Sure, each one is powerful on its own, but together they can save the entire universe from a giant purple bloke with a God complex and a jewellery obsession.

Mindset: The foundation. We've explored how to silence your inner critic, embrace self-compassion, and reframe life's inevitable curveballs. You've learned to take control of your narrative, flipping from victim to hero faster than a reality TV contestant flips tables.

Movement: Your secret weapon. From the humble walk to the sweat-dripping MRT session, you've discovered that exercise is more than just a calorie burner—it's a mental health powerhouse. Plus, it's a lot more fun when you imagine wrestling a kangaroo or chasing your mate Dave with a kettlebell.

Nutrition: The fuel. You now know that eating well doesn't mean giving up everything you love. It's about balance, smart choices, and sometimes just having a bloody good plan.

Your Next Steps
So, what now?

Start small. Pick one thing from each part of this book and make it a habit. Maybe it's starting your day with a gratitude list, taking a daily walk, or swapping your afternoon snack for something that doesn't come from a vending machine.

And remember, it's not about being perfect. You're not a robot. (Unless you are, in which case, welcome to humanity's health manual.) Life will happen, and that's okay. The goal isn't to avoid the storms but to rise above them, armed with the tools you've gained here.

Parting Words
You've got this. And whenever that inner critic pipes up, tell it to just sit the Hell down and shut up. You're the hero of this story, and the world's a better place for having you in it.

Now go out there, live boldly, laugh loudly, and if you ever feel overwhelmed, just remember: life's a bit like wrestling an octopus—it's slippery, unpredictable, and just when you think you've got a handle on things, another tentacle whacks you in the face. But hey, once you stop flailing, you realise you've got the strength to wrestle it into a hug. Everything's going to be just fine.

Slimy, but fine.

About the Author

Hi, I'm Anthony Punshon—fitness trainer, chain tea drinker, and someone who's been through more ups and downs than a squirrel on a trampoline.

Over the past almost 30 years, I've made it my mission to help people transform their bodies and minds, all while trying not to spill my cuppa.

Unlike those trainers who seem to have been born with six-packs and an uncanny ability to flex in every mirror, I started out as the human equivalent of a twiglet. Seven stone, zero muscle, and a wardrobe full of "slightly too big" T-shirts to (unsuccessfully) hide it all.

I've been skinny, I've been overweight, and at one point, I resembled a deflated beach ball with legs.

I've also had my fair share of run-ins with unexpected plot twists. Chronic back pain? Check. Prolapsed disc? Double check. Enough physio sessions to fund a small island? Oh yes. But each setback only made me more determined to crack the code of sustainable fitness and health—and not just for me, but for anyone who's ever felt like they're fighting an uphill battle with a blindfold on.

For over a decade, I ran Sussex's leading transformation studio, helping countless people achieve life-changing results. These days, I focus on helping people achieve extraordinary results through my writing, coaching, and virtual programmes.

My work's been featured in *Men's Health* and other big-name mags, but my real pride comes from seeing people smash their goals—and occasionally (very occasionally) hearing them mutter, "I actually like squats now."

When I'm not coaching or writing, you'll find me drinking enough tea to single-handedly keep the British economy afloat, jamming on the guitar like I'm auditioning for a midlife crisis rock band, or hanging out with the love of my life, my 9-year-old son, who's somehow inherited both my love for fitness and my ability to turn any room into a mini gym. He's always up for a workout, and let's be honest, it's nice to have a training partner who doesn't groan louder than me during push ups.

This book is packed with everything I've learned—strategies, tips, and enough jokes to make your fitness journey a bit more fun. If I can turn things around, you can too.

I've helped thousands of people slash their body fat and tone and shape their muscles through my courses, books, articles, and of course in-person training and consultations.

I'd love to help you too!

You can find out more about how I can help, and get in touch at:

www.anthonypunshon.com

ANTHONY PUNSHON

Printed in Great Britain
by Amazon